In the list of the eighteen Mahapuranas, the 'Linga Purana' is invariably listed as number eleven. But it does not mean that the Linga Purana was eleventh in the order of composition. There are many rituals in the text and these tend to indicate that the Linga Purana was composed much earlier because it contains many legends and stories that date back to much hoary a period. Even though the Linga Purana doesn't conform strictly to the conditions laid down for a Purana to be a Mahapurana, it is, indeed, considered a Mahapurana. It gives the details of Shiva-pooja and Yoga etc. in a most elaborate manner, not found even in the Shiva Purana. It is considered to be a Tamasika Purana. It is divided into two parts—the first part is said to be 'Poorva Bhaga' and the other, 'Uttara Bhaga'. There are one hundred and eighty chapters ('Adhyaya') in the first part and fifty five in the subsequent part.

AF520109

Linga Purana

B.K. Chaturvedi

DIAMOND BOOKS

Publisher : **Diamond Pocket Books (P) Ltd.**
X-30, Okhla Industrial Area, Phase-II
New Delhi-110020
Phone : 011-40712200
E-mail : wecare@diamondbooks.in
Website : www.diamondbooks.in
Edition : 2025
Printed by : Repro (India)

Linga Purana
By : B.K. Chaturvedi

Contents

Preface

In the list of the eighteen Mahapuranas, the 'Linga Purana' is invariably listed as number eleven. But it does not mean that the Linga Purana was eleventh in the order of composition. There are many rituals in the text and these tend to indicate that the Linga Purana was composed much earlier because it contains many legends and stories that date back to much hoary a period. Even though the Linga Purana doesn't conform strictly to the conditions laid down for a Purana to be a Mahapurana, it is, indeed, considered a Mahapurana. It gives the details of Shiva-pooja and Yoga etc. in a most elaborate manner, not found even in the Shiva Purana. It is considered to be a Tamasika Purana. It is divided into two parts—the first part is said to be 'Poorva Bhaga' and the other, 'Uttara Bhaga'. There are one hundred and eighty chapters ('Adhyaya') in the first part and fifty five in the subsequent part.

However, the language of the Purana is quite difficult and the style is rather convoluted. The composition is not as skilled as in the case of many other Puranas. The sentences are much long-winded, and hence the comprehension becomes relatively more difficult. At many places the legends are only referred to in passing reference and that, too, quite repeatedly. In order to present this work is an easy-to-understand and comprehensible language, we have taken recourse to many other Puranas (of the same series) so as to complete the story or the legend. When the legends become repetitive and are well known otherwise, we have even skipped the full story after barely touching the theme of the story. Sometimes after giving the full story the basic idea behind that legend has been given in the marked foot-notes. It has been done precisely for two reasons: One, to make the comprehension logical and second to abridge the ritualistic details which may hinder the stream of thought. The attempt is to give a brief but comprehensive glimpse into this Purana to our curious readers—bred and brought up in a 'computer-logic based' atmosphere.

It is earnestly hoped that this version of the 'Linga Purana'—rendered into English after consulting many of its versions appearing in the original—would reveal the full idea behind this symbol-worship. Lastly the writer of this work wishes to share his gratitude he feels for Shri Narendraji of Diamond Pocket Books whose enthusiasm to revive our culture known no bounds.

—B.K. Chaturvedi

Prologue

Our salutations to Brahma, the creator; Vishnu, the sustainer; and Shiva, the destroyer. We also pray to the sages Nara and Narayana and the goddess of learning Saraswati. We also pay our obeisance to Sage Vedavyasa who made all the sacred texts accessible to us. We are entitled to read the sacred prayers only after saying these prayers.

Once Sage Narada, travelling all over the cosmos unchecked, happened to reach the holy teertha (pilgrimage centre) Nemisharanya. At that time many a great sage had assembled there. They all greeted Narada very warmly and all did obeisance to this psychic son of the Creator. When Narada was duly established on his exalted seat, the sages requested the Sootaji[1] called Romaharshana or Lomaharshana. Getting this request the Sootaji bowed to Naradaji and started recounting the Linga Purana's details while explaining the significance of the Linga. [Linga is the symbol of Lord Shiva who also symbolises the regeneration power of man, allegorically explained by his ever present mount, the Bull. There are several legends that explain how, mythologically, the Linga became the symbol of Lord Shiva. The 'Padma Purana' says that it was the consequence of a curse pronounced by Bhrigu, the great sage. When Bhrigu was sent by the great Rishis (sages) to test who among the three super gods was the greatest, he came to Shiva's abode. Wishing at once to enter, he was prevented by a door-keeper who informed him that as his master (Lord Shiva) was with his wife, it was impossible to enter at present. After waiting for some time Bhrigu's patience exhausted and he said: "Since thou, O Shiva, hast treated me with contempt in preferring the embrace of Parvati, your forms of worship shall be the Linga (phallus) and Yoni (vagina)".]

---

1. There used to be a class of recounters who were generally the off-springs of Kshatriya fathers and Brahmana mothers though they were very learned.

He said that the Linga represented regenerative power of the world. "It is believed to be the origin of all creations."

He said that "the divine essence is known as the Brahman. In the very beginning Brahman was the only entity in the universe. There was nothing else. It was this Brahman who divided himself into three different parts called Brahma, Vishnu and Shiva. Brahma became the creator; Vishnu, the sustainer and Shiva, the destroyer.

"In the very beginning there was only water in the universe. In the water a gigantic egg (Anda) appeared. Brahma emerged from this egg which also contained all the worlds that were likely to be created."

"During Brahma's day, creation flourishes. But during his night there is destruction (Pralaya). When Brahma emerged out of the primordial egg, that constituted the original process of creation (Sarga). But following the process of destruction that takes place during Brahma's night, there is also a periodical process of recreation (Pratisarga). Maheshwara (Lord Shiva Supreme) is the ultimate authority to cause this formal process of Sarga and Pratisarga. The realms with their presiding deities, sages stay during the Sarga and get dissolved in the oblivion during Pratisarga."

According to the Linga Purana, the smallest unit of time is a 'nimesha' which is equal to the time taken in blinking one's eyes. Fifteen nimeshas make one 'Kastha', 30 Kashtas one 'Kala' and 30 Kalas make one Muhurta. One Ahoratra (day-night) contains 30 Muhurtas in all—15 during day and 15 during night. Thus 30 Muhutras make one Ahoratra. One human year makes one 'ahoratra' for the gods. The day part for the gods is called 'Uttarayana' which constitutes six months and the night part of the gods, also of six human months, is called Dakshinayana.[1] Three hundred and sixty human years are equivalent to one divine year. Thus, 12000 divine years are equivalent to 4,320,000 human years which also defines the duration of a Mahayuga. One Mahayuga contains four yugas (eras): Satya Yuga, Treta Yuga, Dwapara Yuga and Kali Yuga. A

1. When the sun tilts northwards between 14th January to 14th July, it is called an auspicious period—Uttarayana—while the period of six months between 14th July to 14th Jan. is called Dakshinayana when the sun tilts southwards.

Satya Yuga lasts for 4000 years of the gods, Treta Yuga for three thousand divine (gods') years, Dwapar Yuga for two thousand divine years and Kali Yuga for one thousand divine year. Thus a Mahayuga is the period reckoned between the starting of the Satya Yuga and the end of Kali Yuga. This way a Mahayuga lasts for 10,000 divine years. However, additionally there is also the intervening periods called Sandhyamsha (twilight zone) between one Yuga and another. This intervening period between Satya Yuga and Treta Yuga is of seven hundred years, between Treta Yuga and Dwapar Yuga of five hundred years, that between Dwapar and Kali Yuga of three hundred years and between Kali Yuga and the new Satya Yuga of five hundred years. These intervening periods make two thousand years. Thus the total span of a Mahayuga is of 12000 divine years.

In terms of human years the Satya Yuga is of 1,440,000 years, Treta of 1,080,000 years, Dwapar of 7,20,000 years and Kali Yuga of 3,60,000. So this Yuga cycle is 3,600,000 human years long. Adding 7,20,000 years for the Sandhyamsha, a Mahayuga is actually of 4,320,000 human years long.

A Manvantara consists of a little over 71 Mahayugas which means that a Manvantara would be equal to 296,720,000 human years. In all there are actually 306,720,000 human years in a Manvantara.

One thousand Mahayugas make up one Kalpa. There are thus 4,320,000,000 human years in a Kalpa. Equivalently, fourteen 'Manvantaras' constitute one Kalpa. Brahma's one day-night (Ahoratri) corresponds to a Kalpa. Brahma's one year is one thousand Kalpas long. Eight thousand such years are one Yuga for Brahma. Also, one thousand of Brahma's Yugas are equivalent to one of Vishnu's days. And nine thousand of Vishnu's days are equivalent to merely one day of Shiva.[1]

---

1. Each Purana pays special emphasis on one of the three Super Gods: Brahma, Vishnu and Shiva. Since this Linga Purana eulogises Lord Shiva, this statement alludes to that spirit of the Purana compilers. One would find the similar glorification of Vishnu in the Puranas dedicated to him. This is why not much emphasis should be laid on the equivalent years of different super gods. Suffice it to say that the ancients had two types of times: one for humans and one for the gods (divine year).

When Brahma's one day ends, the entire universe and all the beings therein are destroyed. But the Super Deities, viz: Brahma, Vishnu, Shiva, remain intact as they are the initiations of the fresh creation. Each cycle starts when there is total darkness and water everywhere. Vishnu remains asleep on this water. [One epithet of Vishnu is 'Narayana' which literally means one who has his abode in water. Impliedly Vishnu signifies life because where there is water there is life—as is corroborated by even the modern science.]

When Brahma's day dawns he begins the process of creation afresh.

In the present cycle Brahma first created three sons through three mental powers (psychic sons. Some accounts say he created four sons). Their names are Sanaka, Sanandana, Sanatan and Sanat-kumara. These were child sages as they started performing great penance right since their childhood. They are always depicted as children. But since they did nothing to enhance creation through the normal process, Brahma had to create another nine sons through his mental powers. Their names are Mareechi, Bhrigu, Angira, Pulastya, Pulaha, Kratu, Daksha, Atri and Vashishtha.

But since they did little to enhance the creation in the normal process, in order to ensure that creation progressed further, Brahma next divided his body into two halves. The male half was known as Swayambhoo Manu, the female half as Shataroopa. These two halves married and had two sons and two daughters. The names of the sons were Uttanapada and Priyavarta and that of the two daughters were Akuti and Prasuti.

Daksha married Prasuti and they had twenty four daughters [The number of the daughters produced by Daksha appears quite variable as some of the mythological accounts claim it to be twenty-four, fifty or even sixty]. One of Daksha's daughters was Sati (or Shakti) who was married to Shiva. But owing to her father's attempt to insult Shiva, she immolated herself in the Yagya performed by Daksha. When Sati died, she was reborn as Parvati, the daughter of the Himalayas. She was again married to Shiva as Parvati.

The Purana says that before starting the process of

creation, Brahma had asked Shiva to help him in the process of creation. "I need your help as I cannot cope on my own," Brahma requested Shiva. Shiva gladly agreed and started to create beings who were more or less his exact replicas. These are eleven forms and known as Rudras. But Brahma was dissatisfied with such creation. "What are you doing?" exclaimed Brahma. "Please do not create immortal beings who are just like yourself. Create beings who are mortal."

But Shiva said he could create only such type of beings. Whereupon Brahma asked him not to create anything. "Instead destroy those that have outlived their utility." Shiva complied but his replicas, Rudra, whom he had already created remained.

The Lingam

During the night of Brahma when all activity had ceased and harmony reigned, Brahma saw Vishnu in his aspect of Narayana floating on a lotus leaf on the waters of space. He asked him who he was. Vishnu, addressing him as 'child', said he was the Creator and Destroyer of all. But Vishnu disagreed and replied that he himself was the creator, preserver and destroyer of all the worlds and that Brahma had been born of his body. An argument took place between them and suddenly they saw a column of fire reaching so far up that it seemed to have no end, and so far down that it seemed to have no beginning. In sheer amazement they ceased quarrelling and decided to find its beginning and end. Vishnu said that he would go down to its source and Brahma said that he would go to its end. They also decided to meet later at its middle point to share their knowledge. Vishnu took the form of a boar with white tusks. Brahma that of a white swan, whose wings were so strong that it could travel as swift as thought and they started the journey. But though they travelled a long time they could not find a beginning or an end to the column. That very moment Brahma espied a flower in the sky and displaying the flower to prove that he had seen the end of that limitless column, he attempted to say that he was superior to Vishnu. Vishnu, unaware of the deceit Brahma was playing, accepted the latter's superiority and touched Brahma's feet. Suddenly as they talked, the air was filled with the sound of the sacred syllable OM (AUM). Sadashiva, the Ultimate Deity, couldn't tolerate Brahma's playing deceitful tactics for his selfish end, appeared in person, through the column and said neither of them was greater than the other, but Brahma-Vishnu-Mahesh, the Trinity was one, each aspect being equally necessary to the whole which he, Sadashiva represented. Sadashiva who appeared from that huge column—the Lingam—also derided Brahma for his attempt to falsely prove his superiority. He cursed him that, henceforth, he (Brahma) shall not be worshipped by the common people, and Vishnu, on account of his truthfulness, shall be the most adored deity, at par with the Ultimate Deity—Sadashiva. That column was the 'Lingam', the symbol of Shiva which is represented mostly by an upright pointed stone, a phallus, placed in a triangular shaped cavity of stone believed to be representing the Yoni (vagina). Both the symbols are shown together which subtly represents the reproduction process of nature.

The Tale of Creation

Continuing the tale of creation Sootaji said: "Aakuti was the elder daughter of Swayambhoo Manu and Shataroopa while Prasuti was the younger daughter. While Aakuti was married to Prajapati Rushi, Prasuti's husband was Daksha Prajapati. Aakuti's progeny were Dakshina and Yagya. Dakshina produced twelve daughters. [As mentioned before] Daksha-Prasuti pair produced twenty four daughters. Out of these thirteen of them were married to Dharma. Another, Khyati, got married to Sage Bhrigu, Smriti to Sage Angira, Preeti to Sage Pulastya, Sambhooti to Sage Mareechi, Kshama to Sage Pulaha, Sannati to Kratu (Sage), Swaha to Agni and Swadha to the Pitragana (the manes).

The pair of Dharma and his thirteen wives produced the following sons: Kaam, Darpa, Niyam, Santosha, Lobha, Shruta, Danda, Samaya, Mahadyuti, Bodh, Apramaada, Vinaya, Vyavasaya, Kshema, Sukha and Yasha.[1] Sage

1. Since the whole description is allegorical, they should be taken as mentioned. As is apparent some of them represent the fundamental emotions of man like Sukha (happiness) etc.

Bhrigu's wife Khyati produced Priyashree who became darling of Lord Vishnu. Prasooti, from her contact with Sage Mareechi, gave birth to two sons named Dhata and Vidhaata. Mareechi's other wife, called Poornamasi, produced four daughters named Tushti, Drishti, Krishi and Aparachiti. The pair of Pulaha and Kshama produced many sons. The pair Pulastya-Preeti produced a son called Kanaka. Sannati and Kratu combination produced as many as 60,000 sons who became famous as Balkhilya Rishis.

While describing the progeny of Agni and Rudra, Sootaji said that Pavaka and Shuchi were the product of Agni and Swaha pair. Their sons and grandsons etc. were forty nine in number. [These are said to be forty nine forms of Agni. Curiously enough, the gases available in a natural form are also 49 in number]. Swadha also produced Maina in the human form whose products were Uma and Hemavati Ganga.

When Brahma had thought of starting the process of creation, he had developed a kind of infatuation which led to the creation of five Avidyas (ignorances) called Tama, Mahamoha, Tamvisra and Andha. Their growth led Brahma to first create beasts and birds. Then with the influence of the Super God he made the creation of the divinities which were followed by creation of man. His first creations were the Sages Sanaka and others, followed by the creation of the Bhrigu, Vashistha, Angiras, Pulastya, Pulaha, Mareechi, Daksha, Kratu and Yogavidya about whose progeny we have already referred.

Knowing about the beginning of the process of creation, the sages assembled in the holy Teertha Nemisharanya asked Sootaji about Yoga which he described in details.

Yoga

Literally meaning union, the generally accepted definition of Yoga is that process by which the individual human soul (Atman) achieves union with that of the divine soul (Parmatman). Lord Shiva is believed to be the originator of this practice. Hence his one epithet being Yogiraja. Shiva is also known as Pashupati. The technique of Yoga that Shiva originated is called Pashupati Yoga. He has his incarnation in every Age—particularly Kali Age. Since there have been twenty eight Kali Yugas so far, there have been his twenty eight incarnations, called Yogeshwaras. Their names are: Shweta, Sutara, Madana, Suhotra, Kanchana, Lokakshee, Jaigishavya, Dadhivahana, Rishabha, Muni, Ugra, Atri, Vali, Gautama, Vedashrira, Gokarna, Guhavasi, Shikhandabhriti, Jatamali, Attahasa, Daruka, Langali, Mahakaya, Shuli, Mundishvara, Sahishnu, Somasharma and Jagadguru.

It is mentioned in this Purana that the Vedavyas in every Dwapar Yuga is an incarnation of Lord Shiva only. Since there have been twenty eight Dwapar Yugas so far, the names of the twenty eight Vedavyas are the following: Kratu, Satya, Bhargava, Angira, Mrityu, Shatakratu, Vashishtha, Sarasvata, Tridhama, Trivrita, Narayana, Tarakshu, Aruni, Deva, Kritanjaya, Ritanjaya, Bharadwaja, Gautama, Vachashrava, Shushmayani, Trinavindu, Raksha, Shaktri, Dheemana, Shatateja, Parashara, Jatukarna, Krishna Dweipayana. [This list doesn't tally with the names of the Vedavyas mentioned in other Puranas.]

Having told about the Yogeshwara (Shiva) and his incarnations, the Sage explained the discipline of Yoga.

Yoga has eight sub-sections which are listed below:

(i) **Yama**: It means total self control including complete command over the senses. Under this category comes the following disciplines:

(a) **Ahimsa**: Not causing violence to any being by one's word, thought or deed.

(b) **Truth**: Never speaking lie and always consciously

following the dictates of the righteous duty or Dharma.

(c) **Asteya**: Never having greed for stealing other's property or rights.

(d) **Brahmacharya**: Maintaining total continence by word, thought or action.

(e) **Aparigraha**: Under no circumstances having a longing for usurping something which is morally not one's due.

(f) **Akrodh**: Keeping total control upon one's temper no matter how provoking the circumstances may be.

(g) **Asooya**: Nursing no jealousy for others no matter how deprived one be yet feeling no grudge against anyone.

(ii) **Niyama**: Leading a well regulated life in total accordance with the Scriptural Dictates. it is further divided into the four sub categories:

(a) **Tapashcharya**: Observing the fasts like the Chandrayasna Vrata for ejecting out of the body all the toxic material that might accumulate in the body.

(b) **Self-Study (Swaadhyaya)**: Reading the holy texts while constantly chanting the following Mantras: OM NAMO BHAGWATE VASUDEVAYA OR OM NAMO NARAYANAAYA and enhancing one's knowledge by devoted study and further brooding and analysing the studied subjects.

(c) **Contentment**: Feeling totally contented with whatever one receives through pure and noble means and having no longing for that which is not achievable by noble means.

(d) **Chivalry**: Or Shaurya means—in this context—winning over one's weakness while keeping total control and fighting fearlessly for a due and honest cause. Keeping the body clean through external applications. In short, keeping the body and mind clean through external and internal control is chivalry in this context.

(iii) **Asanas**: It means sitting in a particular posture with total concentration of one's mind. The following ones are important Asanas or postures. Most of the names of the Asanas are derived from the shape the body takes during the performance of these Asanas. The Asanas are: PADMA, SWASTIKA, SINHA, KUKKUTA, KUNJAR, KOORMA, VAJRA, VARAH, MRIGA, KRAUNCHA, VRISHABHA, NAG, MATSYA, SARVATOBHADRA, VYAGHRA, ARDHACHANDRA, DANDAVAT, SHAIL, MAKAR, VAIKERNICK, STHANU,

BHEEM AND VEER[1].

(iv) **Pranayama**: Sitting at a quiet place and exercising total control over one's exhalation and inhalation so as to find an even rhythm is called Pranayama. It has two sub-categories:

(a) *Agarbha*: Resistance towards inhaling the life breath without any meditation or chanting of some Mantra is called Agarbha Pranayama.

(b) *Sagarbha*: Maintaining the even balance between exhalation and inhalation while chanting some Mantra is called Sagarbha Pranayama. It is further classified into four sub categories:

(i) *Rechaka*: While the Nadi Pingala is situated on the right side of the body, Ida is on the left side. The Nadi that remains in the centre is called Sushumna. While withholding the breath from Pingala and releasing it through Ida is called Rechaka. [In common parlance it means releasing the held up breath].

(ii) *Pooraka*: It is the reverse technique of the earlier variety. Breathing in from Ida and holding it in Pingala is called Pooraka (literally, filling up).

(iii) *Kumbhaka*: Retaining the breath drawn in from either nostril and holding it as long as one can is Kumbhaka.

(iv) *Shoonyaka*: Refusal to draw in breath from outside while holding the breath already inside is called Shoonyaka.

(v) *Pratyahara*: It means making the mind introvert. That is, withdrawing the concentration from outward and fixing it on the inward consciousness or towards the Inner Self (Brahmana) is called Pratyahara. It means cutting off the body consciousness from sensual perceptions and keeping it fixed on the inward activity.

(vi) *Dharana*: The effort of the mind for retaining the inner consciousness and withdrawing it from sensual perception is Dharana. Literally it means holding or retaining an experience.

(vii) *Dhyana*: It literally means meditation. While making the mind concentrated on Lord Supreme after cutting it off from the outward deviations is Dhyana. This is the last stage before Samadhi.

---

1. Most of these asanas are still in practice.

(viii) *Samadhi*: This is the first stage of meditation in which the perceived, the perception and the preceptor coalesce. The famous example of the steady flame of an earthen lamp in a windless chamber explains this stage well.

Thus this Yoga discipline has eight components starting from Yama and ending at Samadhi. It is the stage of Samadhi which is the ultimate meaning of Yoga in which the union between the Paramatman and Atman is realised. Yoga must always be practised in an appropriate place. It should neither be close to a fire nor a cremation ground or a location frequented by wild beasts.

Yoga practice is difficult to master. There are numerous distractions and disturbances that make one deviate from the correct path. One he has to fight always against natural laziness and sloth. Hallucinations, illusions and even nightmares caused by the unholy spirits also appear as hurdles. But one who doesn't get deviated from one's chosen path does get the true bliss akin to god-realisation.

According to this Purana apart from being origin of Yoga practice, Lord Shiva also initiated both Lord Vishnu and Lord Brahma into the most sacred Mantra: the Gayatri Mantra. He also impressed upon the two that "We all three are the part of the same supreme power called Brahman. While Brahma is creator, Vishnu is the sustainer, I am the destroyer of the creation. Hence we should never fight on deciding the matter as who is superior. We are the three aspects of the same power. It is our Yoga that makes the Ultimate Supreme God called Brahman.

A Tussle Between Brahma and Vishnu

As already mentioned, once Vishnu addressed Brahma as "child". This led to the dispute between them as who was greater between them. Despite Shiva appearing with his 'Lingam' to settle it, it had not ceased. When the sages assembled at the Holy Teertha of Nemisharanya and asked the Sootaji for the details, he recounted the following story from the Kalpa famous as the Padma Kalpa:

Following the destruction that ravaged the universe at the end of the previous Kalpa, there was water everywhere and Vishnu kept on sleeping on this water upon his couch made of the coil of the 'Shesha', the Primordial Serpent. As he awoke he found a lotus growing out of his navel. Since he was getting bored he started playing with that lotus which grew out of his navel region. The stalk of the lotus was made of diamonds and it shone with radiance like a brilliant sun.

While Vishnu engaged himself with the lotus he found Brahma appearing. Brahma was surprised seeing Vishnu and asked as to who he was and what was he doing there.

"I am Vishnu", replied Vishnu rather authoritatively, "the Lord of everything. But who are you?", he asked Brahma, "and where have you come from?"

"I am Brahma", replied Brahma with the same authoritative tone. "I am the creator of everything that exists in this universe. Every object that will be created in the universe is already present in embryonic form inside me. If you have any doubt, you may enter my stomach and confirm whatever I say."

Sheer curiosity made Vishnu enter Brahma's body through his mouth. He was amazed to discover the fourteen Bhuvans (realms) of the universe along with the beings who were likely to populate the same. Although Vishnu wandered inside Brahma's stomach for a thousand years, he couldn't find any end to the world spread far and wide inside Brahma. At last he came out the way he had gone in and exclaimed: "I am amazed to see whatever I have seen inside you. But I have more worlds inside me than you have. You may check it personally by entering into my body."

Brahma agreed to this and entered Vishnu's body through the mouth. He wandered for about a thousand years but he couldn't fathom the innumerable realms and reach the extremities of the vast expanse. Meanwhile, Vishnu had closed all the points of exit and Brahma could get no way of coming out. He eventually came out through the lotus that sprouted out of Vishnu's navel and seated himself on the lotus. He thus acquired an epithet, Padma Yoni, which means born through lotus. Moreover, since he emerged out of Vishnu's body, he came to be regarded as Vishnu's son also.

While Brahma was thus seated on the lotus, Shiva arrived there. Since Shiva's arrival created many waves, the lotus started to tremble and Brahma was showered with drops of water. Whereupon, Brahma said: "Please stop shaking the lotus so violently. You are scaring me."

Brahma's this uttering made Vishnu realise his presence. "Who speaks from my navel?" asked Vishnu. "And why does he sound so angry?" "I am Brahma. Don't you remember? You had entered my body and had marvelled at the worlds I had shown you there. You had then asked me to enter your body. But as I did it you closed all the points of exit from inside your body so that I was trapped inside. Then I had to emerge through the lotus growing out of your navel. Now this lotus is shaking so violently that I almost feel unstable. There are enough reasons for me to be angry"

"Pardon me, O great lord," Vishnu said apologetically. "I had no desire to offend you by closing all the points of exit. Please forgive me. And as a token of your friendship, please grant me this boon that henceforth you will be known as my son. But as for the complaints of shaking the lotus, I have no part in it. These tidal waves must have been caused by Shiva's arrival. Let us pray to him and pacify him."

"But who is Shiva?" asked annoyed Brahma, "I am Brahma, the lord of everything. How can any one dare disturb me?"

But wise Vishnu quietened down Brahma and persuaded

him that the two of them ought to pray Shiva. Shiva, getting pleased with these prayers, offered to grant both Brahma and Vishnu boons. Whereupon Vishnu desired the boon that he might always remain devoted to Shiva and Brahma desired that Shiva might be born as his son.

Later on, when Brahma began his task of creation, he was not happy with the beings he initially created. From this sorrow were born the eleven Rudras, the manifestation of Shiva. They were name 'Rudra' because they wept when created[1]. This way Shiva was born as Brahma's son.

[There seems to be some confusion as earlier the Linga Purana has mentioned that Shiva had created the eleven Rudras himself. The story of the Rudras being born from Brahma's sorrow is given in many Puranas in much greater details.]

The Linga Purana next describes the rituals that have to be followed is worshipping Shiva's Linga.

---

1. 'Rudra' is made from the Sanskrit root 'Rud' which means 'to weep'.

The Ritual Worship of Shiva

While telling the sages assembled in Nemisharanya about worship of Lord Shiva, the Sootaji said: "His image is to be placed in this way. Concentrate on his Maheshwara image in the heart, Shiva image at the navel, Chandrachuda Shiva (Shiva with the crescent moon) at forehead. Lord Shankar at the centre amidst the eye-brows. His all the visages fill in up the devotee a sense of bliss.

The objects of his Worship: Then he gave the details of various objects that should be used in his worship.

(i) *Devadaru*: Deva means divine and daru means tree (or wood). A 'devadaru' is a special sort of tree—a typical type of the pine tree that is found upon the hilly terrains like the Himalayas. [Devadaru is a kind of Pine tree].

Many years ago, there used to be a forest that was full of 'Devadaru tree'. In this Devadaru forest there lived many sages with their wives. All these sages were devoted to Lord Shiva and they performed very difficult 'tapasyas' (penance) so as to please him.

Although Lord Shiva was pleased with the prayers offered by the sages, he decided to test the devotion of the sages. Adopting a very ugly appearance he came to that pine-forest. With his complexion being totally dark, eyes terrifying and a completely unclad body, he presented an eerie spectacle. While the wives of the sages began to follow Shiva around, the sages were disgusted. They were chagrined to see their wives following that ugly being. 'Why should they move around that ugly creature?' they thought. They were so charged with disgust that they started using insulting and harsh words to insult that being (Shiva). In no time that creature vanished.

The sages, who were making offerings to Shiva on the advice of Brahma, went back to the creator and told about all that had transpired. But Brahma was angry knowing what they had done. "You idiots!" he blurted out, "Do you know the consequences of what you have done. That ugly creature was no one else but Shiva himself! He was merely trying to test you all and you have miserably failed in that test. He was your gu st and you have treated him so badly. Remember that a guest is a guest, deserving all courtesy and welcome from the host, no matter how ugly and disgusting he may appear. He should be treated with utmost respect and consideration. You all have failed in upholding this age old norm. Perhaps you don't know the story of the sage Sudarshana." Then Brahma recounted this tale:

There was a very staunch and dedicated sage called Sudarshana. He was a strict disciplinarian and the upholder of the age old norms. He also told his wife: "a guest must always be treated well and must never be refused. In fact any guest is like Great Lord Shiva himself. To refuse a guest is tantamount to refusing and insulting Lord Shiva himself."

After some time, the god of righteousness and propriety, Dharmaraja, desired to test the sense of hospitality in sage Sudarshana and his wife: Adopting the disguise of a Brahmana, he came to visit Sudarshana's cottage. Sudarshana was away at that time but his wife treated the guest with great care. She passed the test with flying colours. Dharmaraja blessed Sage Sudarshana's wife that both of them would surely go to heaven.

Now, listening to the story of Sudarshana's wife, the sages were quite annoyed with themselves. They felt as though they had missed a chance of winning Lord Shankar's favour. When they asked creator as to what should they do to get Lord Shiva's favour, Brahma told them the following story of Shveta:

The Tale of the Sage Shveta

Sage Shveta was very much devoted to Shiva. He kept himself busy in praying to Lord Shiva day in and day out. When his life's end came, the god of death came to claim his soul. But Shveta was not at all disturbed at the sight of Yama. He was convinced that death could do no harm as he was Lord Shiva's great devotee. Sensing his end, he started praying fervently to Lord Shiva. While doing so he also started making preparation for the formal worship of Lord Shiva.

"Why are you praying to Shiva now? Your time on the earth", said Yamaraja, "is over and you are now under my control. Why should you start praying to Lord Shiva now?"

Saying no, Yama instructed his messenger to tie Shveta's soul in their inescapable noose to drag the soul to the death's realm. But all of a sudden there arrived Shiva, accompanied by his favourite mount, the bull, Nandi, Parvati and his other hench-persons. At the mere sight of Shiva, Yama fell unconscious. And Shveta was saved. The gods marvelled at this and showered down flowers from the heaven.

"This way," concluded the creator, "Shveta was saved. Lord Shiva is all-powerful and no matter when and how you worship him, if your feeling is genuine, he will always protect you".

Getting the clue from Brahma, the sages again started praying Lord Shiva for an entire year. Pleased by their worship he appeared again in that Devadaru forest but again in his typical guise: his body smeared with ashes and snakes coiling round his neck. His eyes appeared terribly intoxicated with Bhang (a narcotic drug). But they (the sages) were not repelled at the sight and they lovingly bowed to him with their wives. They welcomed Shiva with incense and flowers. Pleased eventually with their guileless emotion this time Shiva granted them the boons of their choice. He also educated them on the wonderful properties of the things that he used to embellish his will. The sages with their wives were delighted to learn the secrets of his Shringar (decor that embellish his body and visage).

[The moral of this story is what is averred by a Latin proverb: "mentem homonis spectato not fruntum" which means judge a person not by his appearance but by his brain]. Dwelling upon the objects Lord Shiva uses to decorate himself, the Sootaji said: "O Sages, this entire copulation-produced creation is the symbol of Lord Shiva. The ash on his body symbolise aversion to sensual delights. The snakes represent the vile tendencies of the beings. Those who worship Lord Shiva with this thought stay away from the travails of this mundane existence. His unclad body represents the total control over the sensual temptation. It was sage Dadheechi who worshipped Lord Shankar in this form to offer his bones for serving the purpose of the divinities." Whereupon the sages asked the Sootaji to recite this tale related to Sage Dadheechi's offering his bones for the sake of the divinities' benefit and the Sootaji obliged.

The Tale of Sage Dadheechi

Sage Dadheechi was the son of Sage Atharva, the compiler of the last of the Vedas, the Atharva Veda, and Shanti. Sage Dadheechi had a friend named Kshupa who was a king. He was a Kshatriya while Dadheechi was a Brahmana. Once the two friends were engaged in a debate as to who was superior—the Brahmana class or the Kshatriya class. While Kshupa maintained that the Kshatriyas were superior, Dadheechi insisted that the superiority of the Brahmana was an established fact.

It was during this period that a serious fight had ensued between the gods and the demons. The demons had become very powerful and they threatened to defeat the gods. The gods sought Kshupa's help and Indra gave his famous Vajra to Kshupa so that he could defeat the demons.

Meanwhile, while arguing on the superiority of the Brahmana or the Kshatriya class, both Dadheechi and Kshupa became so charged as to hurling blows upon each other. Dadheechi struck a blow on the head of Kshupa with his fist. In retaliation, Kshupa struck Dadheechi with the Vajra (thunderbolt) given to him by Indra. He had hurled it so powerfully that it sliced the sage in two parts which caused the sage's almost instant death. But before he could be actually dead, Kshupa called the demon priest Shukracharya and sought his help. Shukracha ya alone knew the art of reviving the dead. [This secret is called 'Mrita Sanjivani Vidya'.] The demon priest reached there and in no time he resurrected Dadheechi.

When Dadheechi was revived to life, the demon chief asked him: "Why don't you pray to Shiva? If you can please the Great Lord, by his grace you will become mortal. It was the Great Lord Shiva who taught me this art of Mrita Sanjivani. Pray to him for getting redemption from all the mundane travails."

Getting so instructed Dadheechi began a very difficult penance in order to please Shiva. Eventually when the

Lord appeared duly pleased, Dadheechi received three boons from him. The efficacy of the first boon made Dadheechi quite prosperous. The second one made his bones as sturdy and strong as the Vajra (thunderbolt) of Indra. And the third boon made him unslayable by any external agency.

Thus fortified Dadheechi rushed to visit Kshupa and gave the latter a mighty kick on his head. In retaliation Khuspa picked up a Vajra and hurled it at Dadheechi's bosom. Although that formidable weapons struck Dadheechi with a resounding whack, yet such was the power of Lord Shiva's boon to Dadheechi that it could cause him no harm. Kshupa was wonder-struck. "How could his Vajra make no dent on Dadheechi?", he was amazed.

Realising that Dadheechi had had his body duly fortified, he resolved that he would pray to Vishnu to obtain still greater powers. He started praying Vishnu very religiously. Eventually Lord Vishnu appeared before him and said: "I am pleased with your prayers. What boon do you desire from me?"

"Please grant me such a boon as could make me defeat Dadheechi", requested Kshupa. "Dadheechi has become very strong by the grace of the boons he received from Lord Shiva", Vishnu revealed. "Hence your this demand cannot be fulfilled. It is difficult yet, nevertheless, I would try."

For the sake of his devotee, Kshupa, Vishnu adopted the form of a Brahmana and proceeded to Dadheechi's hermitage.

"Welcome, great Lord Vishnu", Dadheechi was delighted. "But why have you adopted the form of a Brahmana? Did you think that I would not be able to see through your disguise? Or you adopted this form under the impression that I would not refuse what a Brahmana asked for? Anyway, please shed off this pretence and come in your natural form. Tell me plainly what ever your intentions are. I would be too glad to be of any use to you!"

Thus disarmed by Sage Dadheechi's penetrating sight, Vishnu came in his natural 'four-armed' form and said: "Now I am going to bring Kshupa to your hermitage. All you have to do is to tell Kshupa that you are scared."

Then Vishnu brought Kshupa to Dadheechi's hermitage. But instead of telling Kshupa that he was scared, Dadheechi said: "I am an avowed devotee of Lord Shiva. Hence I cannot be scared of anything in the universe."

Although Dadheechi had not accepted Vishnu's condition. Vishnu had thought Dadheechi's silence meant his accepting the condition. This made Vishnu quite angry and in wrath he readied his famous Sudarshana Chakara. Soon he flung this at Dadheechi. But owing to the boon he had received, the famous discus of Vishnu could make no impact on Dadheechi's body. It, having struck on the chest of Dadheechi, fell harmlessly on the ground.

"Oh amazing!" exclaimed Dadheechi in a mocking vein. "Whatever has happened to great Lord Vishnu's mighty Sudarshana Chakra? Perhaps he should use some other divine weapons. Like Brahmastra........perhaps."

On the other hand, further peeved Vishnu hurled a 'Brahmastra' at Dadheechi. But again no effect on the sturdy sage. Not only that Vishnu used several other divine weapons but none of them could cast any impact on Dadheechi's body. Meanwhile, other gods also arrived there to help Vishnu in his fight with Dadheechi. But notwithstanding the numerous weapons thrown at Dadheechi by the divinities led by Vishnu, Dadheechi stood calmly undamaged. Then seizing his moment Dadheechi picked up a handful of straw and flung this at the gods. As if by magic each of the straws becaming a fire-oozing trident and threatened to incinerate all the divinities present there. The gods panicked and fled in desperation. Meanwhile, Vishnu created several beings who were just like clones of Vishnu. But Dadheechi burnt all of those up. Vishnu next adopted a gigantic and wonderful form. This form, famous as Vishwaroopa, shown the entire universe repositing in his person.

Seeing Vishnu's Universal Form, Dadheechi only laughed. "Who are you trying to overawe?" he asked. "Look at me. You will find the entire universe and all the beings in me I can too play up such illusions. Give up this hallucinatory pretensions. If you really want to fight, let us do so plainly."

At this stage Brahma intervened. He advised Vishnu to pray to the sage instead of fighting with him. When Vishnu prayed he was instantly forgiven by Dadheechi. Then Vishnu also made Kshupa accept the superiority of the Brahmanas over Kahatriyas. Dadheechi also forgave Kshupa. The place where this confrontation had taken place is known as Sthaneshwara.

The Tale of Nandi

As is well-known, Nandi, the bull, is Lord Shiva's favourite mount. Upon being asked by the sages, the Sootaji told them the following story:

Long-long ago there was a sage named Sheelada. In order to get a son he had performed a great penance. After he did it for many years, there appeared Indra before Sheelada and said: "I am pleased with your worship. You may have your boon."

"Please grant me a son, not normally born and who should be immortal."

"That I can't promise", Indra helplessly said. "It is beyond my powers to grant you such a boon. All that I can offer is a mortal son to you. But not immortal one. All that come in this world must die. Not even Brahma can offer anyone an immortal son. Perhaps only Shiva has such powers as he rules over time. He is Mahakaal. For achieving this boon you must pray Him only."

But Sheelada was determined to have an immortal son. So he started worship to please Lord Shiva. Although Shiva is believed to be a god that is reputed to be easily propitiable, in Sheelada's case the poor fellow had to pray even for a thousand years; yet Shiva did not appear before him. Sheelada prayed unmoved and non-stop all this while. Owing to his immobility the termites could build a nest on his body. With the result his body could no longer be seen. The termites ate up all Sheelada's flesh and drunk up all his blood. But undaunted, Sheelada kept on praying, displaying his unswerving devotion to his cause. When he was reduced to merely being a skeleton, Shiva appeared before him. "Enough of your penance", said the Lord. "I know what you desire and I will grant you the son as you desire. I myself will be born as your son at due time. My name will be Nandi."

So declaring Lord Shiva vanished before Sheelada. But he had revived Sheelada's body to pink of health and strength.

Now Sheelada started a yagya to achieve his purpose—the birth of a son. Nandi emerged from that holy fire of the yagya. Nandi was born with three eyes and four arms. He emerged from the fire holding a trident and a mace in two of his hands. His body was wrapped up in an armour made of diamonds. As Nandi emerged, the Gandharvas sang songs to celebrate the occasion while the Apsaras danced to have such an immortal being amidst them. The delighted gods slowered down flowers from above. Nandi, which literally means joy, gave everyone joy. Hence his name Nandi.

However, as soon as Nandi was taken home by his father, all the divine appearances covering his body vanished and he assumed the form of an ordinary human child. Moreover, he forgot all about his divine origin. This made Sheelada somewhat disappointed. But he had no go but to accept the rule of destiny.

Reconciling to the circumstances, he devoted himself to getting his son formally educated. As the precocious child that Nandi was, he became well-versed in all the Vedas and the Shastras (Scriptures) before he was even seven years old.

One day the two gods, Mitra and Varuna, happened to visit Sheelada's hermitage. They were asked to bless the child, Nandi, by Sheelada. But the twin gods exclaimed with a deep sigh, saying: "No amount of blessing can make him survive for long. Despite his body bearing all the auspicious signs he is unlikely to live long. He may not live beyond eight years."

Sheelada was crest-fallen with despair. He was shocked that his 'immortal' son would live for only eight years. In the excess of his agony, the helpless father began to weep. Nandi, the child, couldn't bear seeing his father wailing so helplessly. In desperation, Nandi started to pray his chosen Lord, Shiva. Shiva immediately appeared and learnt from Nandi the cause of Sheelada's agony. At once the Lord declared: "This is all nonsense. Nandi is immortal. My word cannot be false. What the twin gods have said is sheer nonsense. Nandi is immortal and he will always be close to me."

Saying so Shiva took off the necklace of beads he was

wearing and put it round Nandi's neck. As he did so Nandi immediately assured a divine form with four arms and three eyes. That very moment Nandi was adopted as a son of Parvati.

Nandi was made the head of Shiva's henchmen called Gana. He also earned the epithet of being a Ganapati. The ceremony of adoption was celebrated with great fanfare with the gods and Ganapati all reaching there to bless Shiva's son.

The Yugas and the Time Division

The Purana claims that each cycle of Ages have four Ages: Satya (Krita), Treta, Dwapar and Kali Yuga. In the first age, Satya Yuga, people were always happy. All were equal as there were no inferior or superior castes or persons. In that age the climate was always moderate—neither hot nor cold. Hatred and jealousy-like vile sentiments were not known. There was no privation for anybody and hunger and thirst were not felt. (In other words, all were well fed.) The earth yielded enough of natural supplies and mankind lived happily on the earth. The seasons had their own undisturbed cycle and nature was friendly to all the beings. People generally lived on the shores of the oceans and in the mountains. Paap (sin) was non-existent, people were in general meritorious and they were righteous by nature.

However, in Treta Yuga, things started to deteriorate a bit. Clouds formed in the sky and it started to rain heavily. But owing to heavy rains trees began to grow well and people comfortably survived on the natural bounty. By this time the individual slowly turned evil and started to fight over the possession of these trees. Instead of providing sap, the trees began to provide people fruits as much abundantly as to make humans survive on them. Nevertheless, people began to fight over what they received from these trees—fruits to eat and barks to cover their bodies.

However, the longing of the people to possess as many trees as possible made the trees gradually wither away. With the result, the changes in weather also became apparent. Now they had to build houses so that they could protect themselves from the vagaries of weather. In earlier times huge clusters of the trees used to provide people protection. Not only in the Treta Yuga, people developed the art of building houses but they also learnt how to produce cereals through agriculture. The development of animal husbandry and agriculture were the notable features of this Age. Being placed in the land that irrigated itself through rain, they started sowing seeds to reap a harvest of crop. Since fire had also been discovered by this time by the sage Angiras, they also learnt cooking. Of course evils had sprouted to take root upon the earth, they had their concentrated clusters. Like Lanka in the south—the concentrated base of the wild species called demons—which were opposed to agriculture, animal husbandry and other means of civilised living as they still preferred to adhere to the ancient norm of staying very close to nature. But they forgot that human brain is not a static instrument. It always tend to improve upon what it has developed. Thus in Treta, the facility was available to uproot such evil tendencies by going there and destroying them.

It was only from Dwapar Age that human kind started to suffer because of the obscurant evil tendencies that became firmer on this earth. Most evil truants like hatred, jealousy, quarrels and fraudulence became apparent. There developed a group of people which could thrive on these tendencies. Famine and droughts were first felt on the earth in this Dwapar Age[1].

Continuing the narration, the Sootaji said: "The worst is Kali Yuga, when human depravity will reach its nadir. This is described to be the time when the holy men will not be revered. All will neglect the Shashtras and their teachings and people will become more sloth and callous owing to their dependence on mechanical gadgets. People would stoop to any level to derive physical comfort. They would increasingly become selfish and cantankerous. All the people of all the categories will vie for each other's position and the norms of the Shoodras will gain predominance in this

---

1. According to other religious texts, Dwapar was actually the Second Age. Dwapar itself means the Second by Sanskrit grammar. Logically Treta was the third Age by the same etymology. However, according to a legend, it was Vashishtha, the great sage, who altered the two Ages' order. When Brahma asked him to become the holy priest of the most notable dynasty on the earth, the Solar Dynasty, he objected to leaving his realm of calm and quietude in which he could freely worship his chosen Lord, Vishnu. But when Brahma said that the Lord himself would become manifest as a human being in that dynasty (as Ram) and having known that age, Treta would appear after Dwapar, by his psychic powers he altered their order.

Kali Age. As such even the higher caste people will behave like the Shoodras. All disciplines of living will be thrown to dogs. Kings will act like thieves and dacoits who may assume the royal authority unto themselves."

Further dilating upon the evil tendencies of the Kali Yuga the Sootaji told that people will recklessly indulge in money-tending. Their avarice will deplete the earth of its resources, with even pure water becoming the casualty. Life expectancy will be drastically low—merely sixteen years. Love for sensual gratification would make even the father vie with his own son. The only redeeming feature would be: any good deed done in this era would fetch ten time more merit than it would have fetched in any other Age. But this Age would be the shortest among all the ages. The incarnation of Kalki at its fag end will set the order right. Righteousness, care for propriety and adoration for the Brahmana, cow and gods will be re-established. For twenty years Kalki will travel around the earth, destroying the evil and ensuring the protection of the good. Destroying the Shoodra kings and the power wielder he shall resurrect the Vedic order of living once again.

According to this Purana, 'Dharma' is a four-legged existence in Satya Yuga, three-legged in Treta, two-legged in Dwapar and single-legged in Kali Yuga. It is because Dharma loses its one leg in Treta that the process of Yagya was commenced in that Age. Yagya was associated with Daan in Dwapar Yuga while in Kali Yuga the chanting of the 'Name'. It is believed that even if one doesn't offer any 'Daan' (alms-giving) or performs any Yagya in the Kali Yuga, the mere chanting of the Name takes one across the sea of mundane existence.

Geography, Astronomy and Seasons of the Earth

Geography: According to this Purana the universe stands divided into fourteen regions (Bhuvans). Seven of these form the upper regions and seven others constitute the lower (nether) regions. The upper seven realms are: Bhuloka (the earth), Bhuvarloka, Swarloka or Swargaloka (heaven), Maharloka, Janaloka, Tapaloka and Satyaloka. The realms of the nether world are Mahatala, Ematala, Rasatala, Talatala, Sutala, Atala and Patala.[1] Those populate the nether worlds are demons and nagas (snakes). Apart from these there are many hells (naraka) in the universe in which the sinners serve their terms of punishment.

The lower portion of the Mahatala is made of gold with all costly gems embedded on the ground. Herein reside the Supreme Lord. The wise and large-hearted kings like Muchukunda and Bali reside in heavens. The whole of Rasatala is made up of huge boulders while the Talatala realm is made up of sands. While Sutala is yellow blue, Vitala off-white, Atala is dazzling white. The Mahatala spreads to the area of seven thousand Yojanas.[2] It has three divisions: two of three thousand yojanas' magnitude while one thousand yojana form their periphery. In the lower region of this realm resides Vasuki Naga, Virochana, Hiranyaksha and Narkasura. The permanent abode of Kalineni, Purogan, is Sutala.

While continuing the narration the Sootaji said, "the earth is made up of many oceans and mountains. The land mass is divided into seven regions (continents or Mahadweepa) called Jambudweepa, Plakshadweepa, Shalmalidweepa, Kushadweepa, Kraunchdweepa, Shaka-dweepa and Pushkaradweepa. The seven major oceans

1. Some of the names of the nether realms differ from those mentioned in other Puranas.
2. A little more than two miles is the distance known as a Yojan.

(samudra) that surround these land masses are Lavana, Ikshu, Sura, Ghrita, Dadhi and Jala (and Sarpi[1]).

As has already been mentioned, Swayambhoo had two sons: Priyavarta and Uttanapada. Priyavarta had ten sons. Their names were Agridhava, Agrivahu, Medha, Medhatithi, Vapushmana, Jyotishmana, Dyutimana, Havya, Savana and Putra. Following the death of Priyavarta, the earth was divided up into seven regions and seven sons inherited a region each. Agridhara received Jambudweepa, Medhatithis Plakshadweepa, Vapushmana Shalmalidweepa, Jyotishmana Kushadweepa, Dyutimana Krounchdweepa, Havya Shakadweepa and Savana Pushkardweepa. [Although the Linga Purana doesn't clarify as to why Priyavarta's three sons, viz., Agrivalu, Medha and Putra did not receive any share from their father's property, the Vishnu Purana clearly mentions that the threesome, owing to their aversion to material possession, declined to be the claimant. The threesome had eventually became eremite.]

Among these the lord of the Jambudweepa, Agridhara, was a great devotee of Lord Shiva. He was a born hermit possessing undecaying youth. He had nine sons who all proved to be the great devotee of Lord Shankara. Their names were Nabhi, Kim Purush, Dhee, Ila, Raya, Hiranya, Kuru, Madrashwa and Ketumana. Their offshoots were respectively Hemalava, Hemakoota, Naishadha, Ilavritta, Neelachala, Sweta Shramakarna, Malyawana and Gandhamadan. Like his father Agridhara also divided his kingdom among his sons and retired to jungle to pursue his penance. The regions of the divided kingdom are called Varsha.[2]

Nabhi's wife was called Meru. They had a son named Rishabha whose son was Bharat [According to some scholars it is after this Bharat that this part of the Jambudweepa came to be known as Bharata, literally meaning of Bharat.

---

1. This name is not mentioned in this Purana. However, other Puranas mention this name.
2. It may be reminded here that India is the Bharatavarsha part of Jambudweepa. Varsha literally means large section of a land mass. Curiously enough, 'Varsha' means large part of both space and of time by Sankrita Grammar. 'Varsha' (meaning year) conform to this theory.

However some scholars claim that India came to be known as Bharata after the name of the great King Bharat who was the son of Dushyanta and Shakuntala.] Bharat Varsha is the part of the Jambudweepa bounded by the Himalayas in the north and by the ocean in the south. Right in the centre of Jambudweepa is Mount Sumeru—also called Meru—and on all sides of Sumeru are many other peaks. Mount Sumeru is so high that it even touches the solar circle. It is believed to be made up of gold with gems embedded in it all over. It is said to be the abode of many a god. The divine capital, Amravati, is on the eastern slopes of Sumeru. The city abounds with beautiful palaces, bejewelled gates and golden pillars, with crystal steps leading down to limpid pools of clear water. The ponds have beautiful lotus of every hue that can be thought of. At yet another corner of Sumeru is the abode of Agni, the fire-god. This part of the city is called Tejasvini. The abode of Yama is towards the south. This way the whole area has abodes of various gods.

Brahma's abode is also on the Sumeru Mount. It is located right in the centre of Sumeru. A river named Jambu flows past the region. It is said that the name Jambu is acquired by the name of this river.[1] There are many mountain ranges on all sides around Sumeru. The Nilachala mountains are toward north, Shveta mountains further north, and the Shringi mounts still beyond. In the east of Sumeru lie the mountains Jathara and Devakuta. The Nishoda mounts are to the south, the Hemakuta mountains further south and the Himalaya mounts still further away towards the south. The mountains Malyavana and Gandhamadana are due west from the centre mount Sumeru. The mount Sumeru forms the axis-point of the earth around which this planet moves. There are four beautiful lakes (Sarovara) around Sumeru: Arunodaya is in the east, Manasa (or the Lake Manasarovara) towards north, Sitoda due west and the lake Mahabhadra is towards south.

---

1. Botanically this part is called Jambudweepa because it has (or had) the Jambu-Tree in abandant quantity. Jambu is the Sanskrit name for Jamun—a black plum and its fruit. The central part of India still has many Jamun trees.

According to the Linga Purana to the east of Bharatavarsha dwell the Kiratas and to the west live the Yavanas. In Bharatavarsha dwell the various castes of Brahmana, Kshatriya, Vaishya and Shoodra. The hells are located below the underworld (nether realms). There are twenty eight hells in which the sinners pass their terms of punishment. [In actual sense these hells are more in the nature of punishments that the sinners have to remain confined in. This allegorical reference should be taken as it is.]

Astronomy

Whenever the sun moves southwards. its speed is accelerated. When it remains in the Agni Disha (south east) it's noon time. The sun travels one Muhurta time in as many as 31,50,000 yojana. The sun's chariot was built by Brahma himself. [According to this Purana] The name of the twelve months are Madhu, Madhava, Shukra, Shuchi. Nabha, Nabbasya, Isha, U:ja, Saha and Sahasya, Tapa and Tapasya. [This nomenclature of the twelve months is rather unusual as the commonly understood names are Chaitra, Vaishakha, Ashadha, Shrawana, Bhadrapada, Kuaar, Kartika, Aghrayana, Pousha, Magha and Phalguna. These may the names given on the basis of the asterisms rising at the beginning of every mouth and the names given earlier may be the original names].

Two months make on season and hence there are six seasons in a year. The seasons are Greeshma, Varsha, Sharata, Hemanta, Sheeta, and Vasant. According to this account Madhu and Madhava are the months of Greeshma, Shukra and Shudi of Varsha, Nabha and Nabhasya of Sharata, Isha and Urja of Hemanta, Saha and Sabasya of Sheeta and Tapa-Tapasya of Vasanta.

Every season has two Adityas (gods), two sages, two Gandharvas, two Apsaras, two rakshasas (demons) and two nagas (snakes) that ride on the sun's chariot to keep the sun company. Their names along with the seasons are given below:

(a) Greeshma: The Adityas, Dhata and Aryama; the Sages. Pulastya and Pulaha, the Gandharvas:

Tumburu and Narada[1], the Apsaras: Kritasthala and Punjikasthala, the Rakshasas: Raksholeti and Prabeti, the Nagas Uraga and Vasuki.

(b) *Varsha*: The Adityas: Mitra and Varuna, the sages: Atri and Vashishtha, the Gandharvas: Haha and Huhu, the Apsaras: Menaka and Sahajanya, the Rakshashas Pourucheya and Vadha, the Nagas: Takshaka and one other (name not mentioned).

(c) *Sharat*: The Adityas: Indra and Vivasvana, the sages: Angiras and Bhrigu, the Gandharvas: Vishvavasu and Ugasha, the Apsaras: Pramalocha and Arumlocha, the Rakshasas: Sarpa and Vyaghva, the Nagas: Elapatra and Shankhapala.

(d) *Hemanta*: The Adityas: Parjanya and Pusha, the sages: Bharadwaja and Gautama, the Gandharvas: Suruchi and Paravasu, the Apsaras: Gritachi and Vishvachi, the Rakshasas: Ape and Vata, the nagas: Dhananjaya and Irawana.

(e) *Sheeta* The Adityas: Anshu and Bhaga, the sages: Kashyapa and Kratu, the Gandharvas: Chitrasena and Urnayu, the Apsaras: Urvani and Purvachitti, the Rakshasas: Vidyuta and Diva, the Nagas: Mahapadma and Karkataka.

(f) *Vasanta*: The Adityas: Twashtha and Vishnu, the sages: Jamadagni and Vishwamitra, the Gandharvas: Dhritarashtra and Suryavarcha, the Apsaras: Tilottama and Rambha, the Rakshasas: Brahmopeta and Yakshopeta, and nagas: Kambana and Ashvatara.

While the solar chariot is described to be drawn by seven horses, that of the moon is drawn by three horses only. The lunar chariot driving horses are completely white in colour. The sun drinks up the energy of the moon for a period of fifteen days. This fortnight is called Krishnapaksha (the dark lunar fortnight). Then the lunar energy is replenished by the sun for 15 days which is called the bright lunar fortnight (Shukla-Paksha).

---

1. Narada is often referred as a Gandharva although be is believed to be a high sage. Perhaps it was for his love in music—he always carries a lute in his hand—he was included in this category as well.

Mercury (or Budha) is held to be Chandra's son[1]. He rides a chariot that is drawn by eight horses. The horses are greenish yellow and the entire chariot is made of gold. Jupiter also has a similar chariot whose eight driving horses are palish white and eight in colour but that of Saturn (Shani) is made of iron.

The sun is the ruler of the planets as Indra is the ruler of the divinities. The moon is said to be the ruler of Nakshatras (asterisms or constellations) and herbs—all vegetation. All these planets and stars revolve round the Pole Star called Dhruva.

The Tale of the Pole Star (Dhruva Tara)

Dhruva in Sanskrit means something fixed and immoveable eternally. Hence the Pole Star being called Dhruva Tara—a star which doesn't ever move.[2] How this star came to be known as Dhruva Tara is given below:

As has already been mentioned, Swayambhoo (or Swayambhava) Manu had a son named Uttanpada. Uttanpada had two wives caled Suniti and Suruchi. Suruchi's son was Uttama and Dhruva was Suniti's son. But since Suruchi was more beautiful, Uttanpada was more fond of her. Hence his affection more for Uttama than for Dhruva.

One day, while getting into the royal court, Dhruva found Uttama sitting on his father's lap on the throne. Like any other child, he also longed to sit in his father's lap on the throne. When Dhruva attempted to follow suit, Suruchi, standing close by, scolded him sharply saying that he shouldn't covet for the throne since Uttama was its eventual occupant. She also reprimanded Dhruva for trying to get something which was not his.

Dhruva felt hurt. So he went straight to his mother

---

1. Mythologically it is said that once the Moon (Chandrama) eloped with Brihaspati's (Jupiter's) wife Tara and made her pregnant. The outcome was Budha (Mercury). Although much fight took place between Jupiter and the Moon eventually they reconciled with Brahma's intervention. Hence Mercury (Budha) is said to be Jupiter's legal son but his actual father was the Moon.
2. Astronomical researches have proved that even the Pole Star has periodic movement although that period in very long. But for all practical purposes the Pole Star is a fixed star.

Suniti and narrated the whole incident. Hearing it Suniti tried to console his son: "Dear son! One gets in this life in accordance with what one has done in his previous lives. Suruchi and Uttama must have done better deeds in previous lives than what we did to deserve the position they enjoy now. Instead of craving for Uttama's position you should try to improve your lot in the coming life so that you get better position in the next life. If you do good deeds, act righteously and religiously there is no reason why you shouldn't get better position than what Uttama enjoys in this life."

Dhruva took this advice to his heart. He said: "Mother! Your words have given me peace. Now I would strive hard to get the position unassailable by any other being. True, the king loves Uttama's mother more and it is also true that I am not her son. But if I am your son I will show you what I can achieve. I don't crave for occupying the throne. Let Uttama have it. I will achieve a place by my hard work and devotion which may have been unachievable by the highest of the Sages and Seers". The determination in the boy's words was quite apparent. Although Suniti tried her best to dissuade him from going to the forest to perform a severe penance, Dhruva would just not listen to her advice now. He straightaway repaired to the forest which wasn't far away from the palace. When Dhruva reached the denser part of the jungle he met seven sages. He bowed before them and said: "I am Dhruva, the son of Raja Uttanpada and Suniti. I am unhappy and so I have come before you." The sages were surprised and they asked: "Prince! You are hardly five years old. What could be the reasons of your feeling so unhappy at this stage? Moreover, your father is a king and ve y much on throne. Nor you seem to be suffering from any illness. Then, what could have caused as much unhappiness to you as to drive you out of the luxury of the palace to these denser jungles?"

Then Dhruva elaborately told them the reason of his unhappiness. He said that he neither desired wealth nor kingdom. He simply wanted to achieve a position no one had achieved thus far. Seeing his determination writ large on his face, the sages were amazed. Such a firm resolve in such a juvenile mind! But they knew the firmness of the

'Baal Hatha!' They knew that should a child decide to achieve anything, nothing is impossible for a determined mind. So instead of discouraging or dissuading him from performing rigorous penance in the dense jungle, they advised him to worship Vishnu only. While departing the seven sages initiated Dhruva into chanting the famous twelve-syllabled Mantra: "OM NAMO BHAGWATE VASUDEVAYA" which is an unfailing incantation to please Vishnu.

After the sages had left, Dhruva continued his journey towards the desert part of the forest, called Madhuvana[1], on the banks of the river Yamuna. Selecting a neat spot right on the bank of Yamuna under a huge tree, he started his worship of Lord Vishnu, chanting the sacred Mantra non-stop. So intense was his devotion that not many days passed when Dhruva's severe penance began to cause a stir in the divine realm. As has always been the case, Indra got nervous seeing Dhruva's determined Tapasya. He thought as though this boy was also doing all this to get his divine throne. Immediately many kinds of obstructions were devised by the celestials at their king's (Indra's) behest. Not only that Indra made the wild beasts of the jungle come ahead to frighten that small boy. But, undaunted, Dhruva continued to chant non-stop the sacred Mantra with redoubled enthusiasm. In fact the disturbance made his intensity to have the god's Darshan grow more intense!

When the gods found themselves incapable of disturbing Dhruva, they grew panicky. They were now convinced that this small boy had set his eye on something very big. At last, helplessly, they repaired to the shelter of Lord Vishnu and told him about Dhruva's great penance. Without bandying words with them Lord Vishnu assured them that Dhruva's penance won't disturb their position. The Lord knew that such exalted position and material gains were the last thing Dhruva was aspiring for. In fact, Vishnu had allowed the gods to devise all obstructions to Dhruva's worship with two intentions. First, to ascertain the firmness in Dhruva's worship and second, to make the gods realise

---

1. Many years later this region was to be known as Mathura to be established by Lord Rama's brother Shatrughna after killing Madhu demon's son called Lavan, also called Lavanasura. It is, again, a symbolical term as the land had much of Lavan (salt).

that there were other positions much respectable than the rewards the gods could have imagined. Having achieved his purpose he decided to appear before Dhruva. So one fine morning Dhruva found his chosen Lord before himself. Lord Vishnu asked: "Dear child! Have you boon!"

Dhruva opened his eyes and had the Darshan of Lord Vishnu. When he saw Vishnu before him he thought as though his all prayers were answered. He didn't feel like having any specific boon. All his yearnings seemed to have gratified instantly. Nevertheless, Vishnu was so pleased with Dhruva's devotion and selfless dedication that he persisted in granting Dhruva some boon. When the Lord persisted, Dhruva said: "I want to attain a position as might place me at the top of the world—unassailable and eternal."

Vishnu assured Dhruva of his getting such a position. He also told dhruva that in an earlier life Dhruva had been a Brahmana who was devoted to Vishnu. Since that Brahmana's friend was a wealthy prince he desired to get the same position. With the result in this life Dhruva was born as a prince.

However, in this life Dhruva desired no such mundane status or wealth: Lord Vishnu promised to make him occupy such an eternal position in the sky as would make all the big stars and planets revolve round it only. His mother, Suniti, by virtue of her being Dhruva's mother, got also a very high position in the heavens not far from that of Dhruva's own position. [The place of the Dhruva Tara or the Pole Star can be easily identified. Near the Ursa Major (Sapatarshi Mandal) is placed the Pole Star.]

All the stars and planets have as many rays as are able to reach the Pole Star. The middle portion of the sun extends to 9000 yojanas. From the earth, nearest is the Moon. Beyond it is Mercury and beyond Mercury is Venus, beyond Venus is Mars, beyond Mars is Jupiter and beyond Jupiter is Saturn. Beyond Saturn is the Sapatarshi Mandal and the Pole Star is even beyond Saturn.

From the Dhruva Tara is Vishnu's realm which is 2000 yojanas distant from it. He who gets total riddance from all his sins gets a place in the realm of Vishnu.

The Sun is the lord of the planets while the Moon is the lord of all the constellations and the vegetation that grows upon the earth. While Varuna is the master of all water in the universe. Agni is the lord of all material wealth and riches. Daksha is the master of all the Prajapatis (progenitors). Indra is the lord of all the gods. Prahlad, the demon-lord, is the master of all the demons and giants (Daityas). Yama is the lord of all the manes. Rudra rules over all beasts and animals. Shailadika (Nandi) is the master of all the spirits. Yet another Gana of Lord Shiva, Veerabhadra, is the master of all the brave persons. Goddess Chamunda is the ruler over all mothers while Ganesh is the lord of all obstructions. While Uma is the goddess of all women, the Goddess of Vani (speech) is Saraswati and Lord of All is Vishnu. This was the hierarchy devised by Brahma to make the universe run smoothly.

He also made the Himalayas as the head of all mountain ranges, the river Ganga that of all the rivers. He awarded the headship of the trees to Shreepati Tree (Wood-apple tree), to Chitrarath of the Gandharvas & Kinnars, to Vasuki of the nagas (serpents) and to Takshaka of the snakes. The headship of all the elephants was granted to Eiravata, of the birds to Garuda, of the horses to Uchhcheishrava, to lion of the beasts, to the bull of all the cows, to Skanda of all the armed commanders. He made Lord Shiva the ultimate repository of all the Shrutis and Smritis (of the Vedas). The headship of the direction was given to Suvarma.

The names of the suns in various twelve months are: Anshu is Chaitra, Dhata in Vaishakha, Indra in Jyestha, Aryama in Ashadha, Vivasvaan in Shravan, Bhag in Bhadrapada, Parjanya in Ashvin, Twashtha in Kartika, Mitra in Margasheersha, and Sanatan (Eternal) Vishnu in Pousha. Their individual strength on the basis of the rays emanated by them is as follows: Pousha—6000 rays, Anshu—7000 rays, Dhata—8000 rays, Vivaswana—10,000 rays, Bhaga—11,000 rays, Parjanya—9,000 rays, Vishnu—6000 rays—which indicate their heat intensity. During the summers the sun has golden hue, during the rainy season white, during autumn copper-like and during winters darkish red.

Apart from the Sun and the Moon, the other known planets are Mars, Mercury, Jupiter, Venus and Saturn. Skanda is the presiding deity of Mars, Narayana of Mercury, Shiva of Venus and Lord of Death, Dharmaraja (Yama) of

Saturn. All these planets have Sun as their lord.

Those which never decay—among the celestial bodies—are called Nakshatra. Those which move across the sky are called Tara. The planets are called Graha because their influence possesses the being. While the sun (Aditya) is the son of the divine-mother Aditi (hence the name). Mercury of the Moon, Mars of the Earth, Jupiter (Brihaspati) of the sage Angiras, Venus (Shukra or Shukracharya) of the sage Bhrigu, Shanichara (Saturn) of Viswana Dyava (Sun). Bhauma (Mars) is also said to be the son of Rudra.

Among the most auspicious asterisms is Sharmishtha (Dhanishtta), between the Ayana (the solar tilt on the axis) is Uttarayayan, among the seasons in Shishir (cold winter) among the months are Margsheersha.[1] According to this Purana a Yug in the general sense is of five years—stretching from Dhamishtha to Shrawana. The auspicious fortnight is Shukla (bright half), the tithis Pratipada and Rudra among the Muhurtas.

1. Some of these auspicious asterisms, seasons, months vary from that given in the holy Bhagwatgeeta. According to it the most auspicious month is Margasheersha but the best season is spring or Vasanta.

The Process of Normal Creation

Getting the details about various planets and much idea about geography, the sages assembled in the holy teertha of Nemisharanya asked the Sootaji to tell about the creation created through normal copulation between a male and female called 'Maithuni Shrishti.'

In started with Daksha, one of Brahma's psychic sons. Daksha had married Prasooti. This union produced five thousand sons known as the Haryashvas. But the sage Narada came and told the Haryashvas that there was nothing to be gained by being addicted to material pursuits. They would be better off if they went away to meditate. Persuaded by Narada, the Haryashvas went off to meditate and have never been heard of since. Next Daksha and Prasooti had produced a thousand sons named the Shavalashvas. But Narada made them also averse to mundane attractions. Eventually they also treaded their path to the jungles to meditate.

At Brahma's inkling Daksha and Prasooti had produced sixty daughters. Ten of them were married to Dharmaraja (Yama), thirteen to the sage Kashyapa and twenty seven to Chandra.

The thirteen daughters of Daksha that were married to Sage Kashyapa were, Aditi, Diti, Arishtha, Surasa, Muni, Surabhi, Vinata, Tamra, Krodhavatsala, Ila, Kadru, Tvisha and Danu. [These names vary from Purana to Purana. Quoted here are those that have been mentioned in the Linga Purana.]

As explained earlier, Aditi's sons were known as Adityas. Their names are those that have already been mentioned while naming the twelve forms of the sun like Indra, Dhata etc.]

Daksha's second daughter Diti (the mother of the Daityas) had two sons, Hiranyaksha and Hiranyakashyapu. His another wife Danu (the mother of Danava) had a hundred sons, chief amongst whom was Viprachitti whose prominent sons were Rahu and Ketu. Daksha's another wife was Tamra, the mother of all the birds. Vinanta, Daksha's another wife, had two sons: Arun and Garuda. While Arun became the charioteer of the sun, Garuda became the king of birds. Daksha's wife Surasa was the mother of snakes (Sarpa). [Most of the other Puranas claim that Surasa was the mother of Rakshasas (demons)]. Kadru gave birth to snakes (nagas). Chief among the snakes were Ananta (also called Shesha), Vasuki and Takshaka. They also claim that Krodhavasha was the mother of Rakshasas and Surabhi gave birth to all cattle. Muni was the mother of the Apsaras and Arishta was the mother of the Gandharvas. From Ila were born the trees and herbs and from Trisha were born the Yakshas.

[The confusion regarding various beings' origin occurs due to the various Puranas giving different names. Even in this Purana, although Garuda, a bird, is said to have been originated by Vinata, Tamra is described as the mother of all birds. Similar discrepancies keep occurring became these Puranas have not been uniformly edited. For the right reference to their origin, the best and most authentic source is the Mahabharat. In order to let the readers realise this difference, we have given their reference as given in this Linga-Purana].

Sage Kashyapa started these creations in order to populate the newly created world and continue his lineage.

According to this Purana, Sage Kashyapa had two sons in the beginning. Their names were Vatsarar and Aasita. Vatsara had two sons named Raitya and Naidhruva. The daughter of the sage Chyavana, Sumedha, became wife of Naidhruva. On the other hand Aasita had Sandrilya and Deval as sons.

In the same order in Treta Yuga Trinabindu was born as the son of Dambha who himself was son of Narishyanta. His daughter Ilavita was married to sage Pulastya. His son was Vishrwa. Vishrwa had four daughters. One of them was Vrihaspati's daughter Devavarnini. Two other wives were daughter of Malyavana and one, the daughter of Mali, Kaikasi.

The union of Devavarnini and Vishrwa produced Vaishravana who later came to be known as Kubera. The union with Kaikasi produced Ravana, Kumbhakarna, Vibhishana and a daughter named Shoorpanakha. The union with Pushpotkata produced Mahodara, Prahasta, Mahaparshva and Khara, as also a daughter called Krimbhunasi. Bala produced Trishara, Dushana and a daughter Malika. In this entire family Vibhishana was most righteous and religious-minded.

In the Sage's lineage, during the Manvantara, Vaivasvata Manu, Kritu was issueless. All the sons of the sage Atri were collectively called Aatreya. Brahma's other psychic sons were Kaashyapa, Narada, Parvata and Anuddhata. Meanwhile, Vashishtha and Arundhati pair produced 100 sons. It was Goddess Kali who inspired Parashar to get a son, famous Krishna Dwaipayan, who came to be known as great Sage Vedavyas later on.

Interrupting the Sootaji's narration the sages wanted to know about the story of Krishna Dwaipayan's birth and the Sootaji obliged.

The Family of the Great Sage Parashara

Long long ago there used to be a Rakshasa named Rudhir and a king called Kalmashapada[1]. The king's body was possessed by a demon. Hence his being called Kalmashapada ('with dirty feet') although he was actually sage Vashishtha's son, Shakti.

[As a matter of fact, king Kalmashapada belonged to the Ikshavaku Dynasty. He had once gone to the forest and had become very thirsty. While looking for some water, he met Shakti. Since the path was too narrow to allow two persons to pass simultaneously, they developed altercation. But Shakti insisted that being a Brahmana he should be given priority. Angered by his insistence, Kalmashapada struck Shakti with the whip and Shakti in turn cursed the king that he could become a Rakshasa. Kalmashapada's first act after becoming a Rakshasa was to eat up Shakti and his hundred brothers].

This way Sage Vashishtha had lost all his sons. It was a great jk.,kshock for him to bear. He and his wife Arundhati became so much disturbed that they decided to end their life by jumping off from a high hill.

But the earth never wanted to lose such a learned and noble sage this way. She immediately adopted the form of a woman and broke the noble couple's fall. Then she also requested: "Please do not try to kill yourself this way. You are needed by the world."

Shakti's wife also heard the earth say this way. She also tried to dissuade her father-in-law from committing suicide. She informed her father-in-law: "I am expecting. If the two of you kill yourself who will look after the son when he is born? He is, after all, your son's son! Please stay alive for the sake of your about-to-be-born grandson."

While this conversation was continuing, the child in Shakti's wife's womb started to recite the Richas of the

1. The story of Kalmashapada has already been given in the 'Markandeya Purana' of the same series.

Vedas. It was so amazing that at first Vashishtha could not believe this sound of Vedic recitation to be coming from his son's wife's womb. But Lord Vishnu appeared and told the sage: "O Sage! You will have a grandson who will bring glory to your line. He will be a great devotee of Shiva. It is he who is reciting the Vedas. Please stay alive for his sake."

Eventually Vashishtha agreed. In due course, shakti's wife—named Adrishyanti—gave birth to a son who came to be called Parashara.

When Parashara grew up, one day he asked his mother. "Who is my father? Why do I do not have a father like all my companions have?"

"Your father Shakti was eaten up by a Rakshasa", replied Adrishyanti.

"What, eaten up by a Rakshasa?" Parashara was shocked. "Now I shall avenge his death. I will pray to Lord Shiva and through my rigorous Tapasya I shall attain great powers. And having acquired those powers I shall burn up the entire universe. There is no point of retaining an evil universe in which the noble sages—like my father—are eaten by the demons."

But Vashishtha impressed upon Parashara that such a blanket destruction of the diverse was quite unwarranted. "Why should you seek destruction of the entire universe to avenge for your father's murder by just one Rakshasa? You may seek that Rakshasa's destruction by all means but why destroy the whole world?"

Getting this advice Parashara resolved that he would use his powers to have all the Rakshasas destroyed.

With this determination Parashara started to pray to Lord Shiva. Propitiated by these prayers he granted Parashara some amazing powers. With these powers, Parashara got to see and talk to his dead father. And he used these powers to try to exterminate the Rakshasa clan as such. But, Vashishtha, the noble sage with the universal vision, again dissuaded his grandson. "There has been enough of killing. Even if your father and my son was killed by a demon, it was written in his destiny. The Rakshasa was only an instrument to have his destiny get that result. So stop killing the Rakshasa any more. This blind anger serves no purpose except breeding more hatred and vengeance.

Parashara saw the sense in his grandfather's teaching. He stopped that Rakshasa-destroying Yagya. Vashishtha was happy that his grandson could curb his anger. He blessed him that soon he would become well versed in all the Shashtras and the sacred knowledge. Vashishtha also predicted that he (Parashara) would compose the Purana Samhita and the Puranas. [Although Puranas were compiled by Sage Vedavyasa, the illegitimate son of sage Parashara, it is quite possible that it was Parashara who might have started the gigantic project to be completed by his son.]

Sage Parashara And Sage Bhrigu: [In some of the versions of the Linga Purana, this story is also mentioned. Even though it may be apochryphal, yet since it contains matter of general interest, it is being included in this work.]

Parashara was a precocious child. Having received Lord Shiva's boon—and guided by his grandfather Vashishtha—he became quite learned. In no time be mastered not only the Vedic literature but also developed the discretion to sift what is good and what is bad for man. While he was continuing his studies, he heard that Sage Bhrigu was also developing an astrological Samhita which might make man aware of the results in every moment of his life. When Parashara heard about it, he developed curiosity to meet Sage Bhrigu.

He asked Sage Bhrigu: "O Great Sage! I hear you are developing an astrological Samhita which is unprecedented in its importance and consequence. Will you care to enlighten me about it?"

"Dear Parashara", replied Sage Bhrigu in a patronising manner, "You have heard right about my Samhita (a sort of pandect). I tell you why have I developed it."

Then he explained the genesis of his much famed Bhrigu Samhita.

Astrologically it is believed that a normal human life span is of 120 years. It is believed that after 120 years (should a man survive) the planetary configuration starts repeating itself. Since the planetary configuration decodes the course of destiny for the human being (by the astrological belief), Bhrigu, a great mathematician himself, made a huge collection of horoscopes having prediction for every native's total life span. "This way", explained Bhrigu. "man would know everything about his past, present and future like the back of his hand."

When Parashara heard it, he said: "O Sage! By developing this kind of Samhita you are not doing any noble job. On the contrary, you are making human life a miserable existence. For if every man knows what lies in store for him every second, not only his life will become a burden but, in that stage, man would be stepping into God's domain. Why would he worship, do any noble act if he knows what he is going to get eventually? This way, I don't think it would serve any useful purpose in human existence. It is better if you destroy this work."

This remark enraged Bhrigu so much that he began to cast a deadly curse on Parashara. But Brahma and other gods intervened. Although they had realised the great sense in what Parashara had said, yet destruction of that Bhrigu Samhita might have meant all the great labour that Bhrigu had put in preparing that unique pandect going just waste. At last at the divine intervention, Parashara, who had cursed that the Bhrigu Samhita's results would not be correct at all, decided to modify his curse by saying: "the prediction about the past would always be correct by the Bhrigu Samhita.[1] But future may or may not be correct y predicted."

Sage Vedavyas's Birth

Long ago there dwelled a king in Chedi Pradesh, named Upanichara, who was of a very religious temperament. He believed that it was God who made this world run the way it did. He had a beautiful wife called Girika. She bore five brilliant sons for the king. Once the king had gone for

1. This is an ancient astrological collection of the horoscopes which is still available at only given places in India (like in Hoshiyarpur in Punjab and in Varanasi in UP). He who is desirous of knowing about his life goes to these centres with his horoscope which is tallied by the huge collection of horoscopes available there. Should it be tallied, the revelation about one's past is normally so correct that they would tell even the name of the native with the help of the collection they have. But there is no guarantee about these Bhrigu Samhita Purohits foretelling so correctly about the future of the native—the person who wants to know about his life through that Bhrigu Sumhita.

hunting and in the jungle he missed his wife so much that he ejaculated uncontrollably. In order to save his seed he collected it in a leaf-cup and ordered his pet falcon to go and have it deposited into his wife's vagina. This way he sent the message to his wife that she must conceive. But as the falcon was taking it, another big bird thought it to have been some edible. So it swiped at the cup, making the seed fall into the river.

It was exactly at that moment a divine danseuse Adnika was swimming in that river, sexually charged greatly. She requested a Brahmana lost in meditation to have sexual union with her. But when the determined Brahmana didn't respond to her overtures, she came as much close to him as to caress his body. This made the Brahmana blow up in rage and he cursed the Apsara to become a fish. But when she repeatedly requested him to modify his curse, he relented: "You shall be released from that form and shall regain your original form when you are able to produce a human being from your womb."

Meanwhile, the seed of the king had fallen into the river. This fish (danseuse) drank it and she conceived also. After ten months, that fish was netted by a fisher-man. He was surprised to see so fat a fish. In greed he tore apart the fish's stomach and out emerged from it two human figures—one boy and the other a girl. While the boy was entrusted to the king's (state's) custody, the girl was given to the fisherman. When she grew up, this girl, having a typical fish like smell ever emanating from her body, began to help her adopted father in his work. Her father's main occupation was to row the boat across the river (Yamuna) and help the people cross the river on payment. Dwelling on the bank of the river Yamuna the father and the daughter earned their living this way.

Once the great sage Parashara happened to reach there in the process of his visiting all the holy spots. When he reached the bank of that river Yamuna, the boat-man, Nishad, was having his food. When he saw him willing to cross the boat, he asked his daughter to do the needful on his behalf. While sitting in the boat the sage was captivated by that (fish-) girl's unusual beauty. He immediately desired physical union with her. But she deterred him, reminding him of his high lineage. But the sage was so sexually charged that he took that girl into his lap. Although the fish-like smell emanating from that girl (named Satyavati) did discourage him from proceeding on the amorous path, the sage used his yogic powers to make her body radiate a sandalwood like fragrance. When the girl objected to their capulating during the day time with many people looking on, the sage created such a matt-screen of cloud that they became invisible to the outsiders. At last Satyavati said: "O Sage, after enjoying my youthful body you will go away. What will I do if I conceive with your seed in me? Can I face my society? Won't the people cast aspersion on an unmarried girl getting pregnant? What, then, shall be my future?" Whereupon, the sage blessed her: "My copulation with you won't sully your maidenhood. You shall still remain most comely and desirable maiden. It is the will of the Providence which made me desire you even though I have withstood the advances of most beautiful damsels in the past. And rest assured, with my union you will beget a brilliant and most intelligent son whose rearing up won't be the duty of you or your father."

Having assured her this way Parashara copulated with her. After that he took the drip in the river Yamuna and left to complete his remaining pilgrimage. After his departure, at due time, the girl (Satyavati) gave birth to a robust and brilliant son on an island who later came to be known as Vyas Krishna Dwaipayan (Vyas, the Dark born on an island). As soon as he was born, he showed the qualities of a precocious child. As he came of age he left his mother to return to her many years later as the most dignified scholar[1] of the earth of his era.

[After Parashara's story the Linga Purana catalogues the kings of the solar and lunar dynasties. Since these are better given in the other Puranas which we have included in our series, we are not giving them here.]

1. Parashara is said to be the father of Indian astrology. His 'Vrihat Parashara' is reckoned as the bible of Indian astrology. Being the grandson of Vashishtha—the arch moulder of the Indian values—and father of Vedavyas, Parashara represents the quintessence of Indian brilliance.

The Tripura Destruction

There was a very powerful demon called Tarakasura who oppressed the gods. He was eventually killed by Skanda, (or Kartikeya) the elder son of Shiva and Parvati.

Tarakasura had three sons named Vidyunmali, Tarakaksha and Viryavana. When they found that their father was slain through a conspiracy[1] hatched by the gods, in order to avenge their father's death, they began to undertake a very difficult penance. This they did to gain the desired boon from Creator, Brahma. For a hundred years they meditated standing on one leg only. Then for a subsequent 1000 years they lived on air and meditated with total concentration. Then they stood on their heads and meditated on this posture for another 1000 years. Eventually Brahma, propitiated by their Tapasya, appeared before them, asking them to have the boon of their choice. "We want immortality", said the three sons of Tarakasura.

"That is not possible", declared Brahma, adding, "everyone who is born must die. This is a universal law. Ask for something else instead." "Very well then", said Vidyunmali, Tarakaksha and Viryavana, "Grant us the following boon. Let three forts be made. The first one of gold, the second of silver and the third of iron. We will live in these ports for about 1000 years. After this period the forts should be united and they should become one impregnable citadel. Then it should be called the Tripura and we may die only when some one be able to destroy this citadel with a single arrow. Make it our destiny."

Although Brahma was amazed to find them seeking such an elaborate boon, bound by his commitment he condescended to say: "So be it."

Getting the desired boon the three demons sought the services of the architect of the demons, Maya Danava to have their demands fulfilled. Maya Danava made the first

---

1. The story of Tarakasura's destruction has not been given in this Purana. But it is available in other Puranas of the same series.

fort of gold in the heaven, the second of silver in the high skies and the third of iron on the earth. While Tarakaksha had the gold fort, Viryavana the silver one and Vidyunmali that of iron. Each of the forts was as big as a city having many Vimanas (aerial vehicles) and other vehicles for their comfort. Now ensconced in these forts the three sons of Tarakasura felt quite powerful. They soon populated these forts with the beings of their choice and began to live well.

Soon their enhancing power became an anathema to the gods. They first went to Brahma with their complaint of his abetment in letting the demons enhance their power. But Brahma pleaded his innocence as he was bound by the law of nature. Then the gods sought the help of Lord Shiva. But Shiva said that the demons were doing nothing wrong and as long as this was the case he did not see any reason for the gods feelings so disturbed. At last the gods went to Vishnu who gave them the following piece of advice: "If the demons were doing nothing wrong the gods must plan in such a way as to induce the demons into doing something wrong. Make them commit some sin so as to be deserving punishment. For unless the demons commit it they cannot be punished." When the gods further asked him to devise some means to achieve this very end, out of his mysterious powers. Lord Vishnu created a man. This man's head was clean shaven, his clothes faded and he carried a water-pot in his hands. He covered his mouth with a piece of cloth and he approached Vishnu. "What have I been created for?" asked the mysterious man.

"I will teach you a religion completely against the Vedic norms. You will then get the impression as though there is nothing like hell or heaven and all the good and bad things exist till one survives on this earth. You will believe that rewards and punishments for deeds committed on the earth are not meted out after death. Now go to Tripura and teach demons this lesson[1]. You must keep on goading the demons

1. The gist of this religion given herein reveals as though it defines the religion taught by the other offshoot of the Sanatana Dharma like the Buddhism and Jainism. This makes it apparent that even the Linga Purana was compiled when these faiths had made their advent and were on the decline which was hastened by Adi Shankaracharya's attack on these faiths to re-establish the Hindu (Sanatana) Dharma after blowing away the cobwebs of ignorance which had earlier let the other faiths dominate over it.

to commit sins so that they be totally dislodged from their righteous path. Only then we can devise a plan to dislodge the demons from their stronghold, the Tripura."

That mysterious man did exactly what he had been asked to do by Lord Vishnu. He was also assisted by his four disciples. They together went to a forest near Tripura. There they opened their pseudo hermitage and began to preach the faith as advised by Lord Vishnu. Since they were trained by the Blessed Lord Vishnu himself, their lessons were proving quite convincing. Soon they had many converts as their followers. Meanwhile, the divine sage Narada was acting as their publicity agent and it was he who first carried the news of advent of a novel faith to Vidyunmali.

"O King", said Narada, "Very close to your capital has been established a hermitage by the preachers of a novel faith. I have never heard any one teaching any faith with such conviction and clarity. As a matter of fact, I, myself, am on the verge of getting converted to these teachings".

Vidyunmali was impressed. Like all noble kings he, too, believed and reposed respect in all that the divine sage said. Soon, following Narada, he, too, was converted to the new faith. Getting the hint from their brother Vidyunmali, Tarakaksha and Viryavana also followed suit. With the result, the demons ceased respecting the Vedas and worshipping the old deities. They also grew averse to even worshipping the 'Linga'—a symbolical manifestation of Lord Shiva himself. This news was magnified manifold by the gods. Led by Vishnu the other gods went to Shiva and began to pray him fervently. When Shiva appeared they told him that the demons had how become evil and hence they should be destroyed. "They have grown as much audacious as to stop even worshipping your symbol, the Linga."

Naturally, Shiva was enraged. In the fit of anger he agreed to destroy the demons along with their citadel, the Tripura. Shiva then summoned Vishwakarma and asked him to make a suitable chariot, bow and arrows. Lord Shiva's chariot was made entirely of gold. Brahma himself became the charioteer and he drove the chariot—with fully armed Shiva seated in it—towards the demons' citadel. The other gods also accompanied Shiva with divine weapons.

It was about this time that the stipulated time of their (the demons') stay in those citadels was drawing to a close. Hence, soon, the three forts coalesced into a single mighty fort. Deeming the opportune time having arrived Shiva set his divine weapon called 'Pashupati Astra' to his bow and shot it at that mighty citadel. The arrow struck at the fort and burnt it up into ashes in a trice.

With the demons' citadel destroyed the gods rejoiced but that mysterious person with his assistants came to ask about his future. Brahma, after consulting Vishnu, told them: "You may stay into the oblivion till the last phase of Kaliyuga when you can grace the earth again."

The Ominous Indications and Dream-Analysis

The Linga Purana mentions some ominous signs which indicate impending death for the one who sees them.

A person who cannot see Arundhati Nakshatra (Constellation) [also called Ursa Majoris], the Pole Star or the Milky Way [our galaxy, also called Akash Ganga] may die within one year's time. A person to whom the radiance of the sun seems to be diminished will die within eleven months. One who dreams of vomiting gold or silver will die within ten months. He who dreams of golden trees, cities of the Gandharvas or ghosts or demons will die after nine months. If one suddenly puts on or loses weight, one may live for eight months. If a person walking bare-footed leaves an incomplete footprint on dust or mud may survive for not more than 7 months. Should a crow, vulture or dove alight on one's head, one may live maximum for six months more. A person who is surrounded by crows when he walks or a person who is surrounded by dust does not live for more than four or five months. Such is also the case with the person who sees his reflection naturally distorted. A person who hears thunder when there are no clouds in the sky or a person who sees a rainbow in the water has but three months to live. If the reflection is incomplete or if the reflection has a severed head, that person may not survive for more than a month. Anyone having his body reeking the smell of the dead bodies may die within fifteen days. If anyone sees smoke billowing out of his head, he may not survive for more than ten days. If one sees himself sitting in a chariot drawn by bears or moneys towards south, one may die soon. He may die immediately if he sees himself singing or dancing while travelling this way. If one sees himself getting submerged in a cesspool of mud (quagmire) one must deem his death to be nigh. If one sees the warriors clad in dark clothes coming charging upon oneself he may die within seven weeks. Should one get up at the stroke of dawn to find jackals greeting him, his death will be quite close. When one extinguishes a lamp but finds the smell of burning lingering in the air which may appear unbearable, one may also die soon.

Following views beheld in dream are not only auspicious but forebode well for the viewer: drinking liquor or wine in the dream, seeing one's body being consumed by insects and mosquitoes, one's body getting defiled by the touch of filth or faeces or blood; seeing oneself eating curd and rice, getting covered with white sandalwood-paste, beholding oneself wearing ornaments or beholding a person well decorated, seeing a Brahman—cow—king—the moon under a canopy, beholding a fully caparisoned bull or snow-clad mounts, seeing one climbing atop a banyan tree or the fruit-laden trees, beholding one's glasses or the garlands floating on water. All these views forebode gain of wealth or money or listening happy news or getting well from a disease.

However the following spectacles are held inauspicious: seeing one climbing atop the pillar of Yagya/a neem tree, receiving oil, cotton or iron in any form; playing oneself in gay abandon, wearing a red-cloth, attempting to change the course of a stream or a river, eating cooked meat. Any such view in the dream foretells the onset of some trouble.

If one sees a moving vehicle [like a car, tonga rickshaw etc.] it is held to be a good omen. Should one behold a rising sun in one's dream it augurs well for the person. In general beholding anything black in the dream is held inauspicious but beholding anything white forebodes a happy news. Beholding cereals is also good. If one sees one's hair falling down it is decidedly a bad omen. Seeing one's hand amputed is also very bad sign. If one beholds a dream right at the dawn or just before leaving one's bed, that dream would show its effect within a week. The effectiveness of a dream is judged in the following manner.

(a) Seen in the early part of the night: effect will manifest itself in 6 months' time.

(b) Seen in the middle part (second phase or 'Dweetaya Prahar') of the night: effect will manifest itself in 4 months' time.

(c) Seen in the third part (Triteeya Prahar) in the

might: effect will manifest itself within three months time.

(d) Seen in the fourth part (Chaturtha Prahar) in the night: the effect will manifest itself within two months time.

This way the dream will show its effect progressively as the dreamer dreams closer to the dawn.

The way to nullify the evil effects of the dream is to 'sleep over' it again and tell about it in details to others. In case the dream is auspicious the dreamer should not sleep after seeing it and should not either disclose it to anyone till it manifests its favourable effect.

The Story of Demon Jalandhara

Once Indra went to Mount Kailash. Drunk in the wine of his pelf and position he saw Lord Shiva there. But as he was brimming with insolence he failed to recognise Lord Shankar. Not only that, he asked the Yogi (Shiva) to get away from his path and when the latter refused he even tried to hit him with his Vajra (thunderbolt) on his head. As the Vajra hit Shiva a deadly fire had hurst forth from his head. It rushed toward Indra with great intensity. Then only Indra could realise what felony he had done. He repeatedly apologised and managed to pacify Shiva—an easy-to-please God or 'Aashutosh' even otherwise. He requested Shiva to direct the fire towards ocean. As Shiva directed the fire towards ocean, from its impact on the water surface was born a boy. Since he (the boy) had emerged from water he came to be known as Jalandhara.

[Another sto y of Jalandhara's origin claims that when Brahma tried to quieten that delinquent boy, the boy tugged so hard at Brahma's beard that water (Jala) came out of Brahma's eyes. So Brahma gave the name Jalandhara (he who carries water with him) and granted him the boon that for everybody else he was immortal and only Shiva (the boy's progenitor) could kill him.]

Thus empowered by the boon from the gods Jalandhara became quite powerful. He defeated all the gods including Indra with his might. Then he challenged Vishnu to a duel. Although the duel lasted for some time, eventually Vishnu, too, met his match.

Having achieved victo y over the top gods Jalandhara told his companions, the other gods: "I seem to have defeated everyone that is there to fight with or could challenge my authority. Now the only one left is Shiva. Let us go out and thrash this Shiva also along with his companion like Nandi and Ganesh."

Receiving this command the demon army trooped to Shiva's abode. As he confronted Shiva, the latter asked:

"What do you want? What for have you come to Kailash?"

"We have come here to fight with you", thundered Jalandhara.

At that point Shiva inserted his big toe into the ocean and started to churn the water. From this churning, the terrible weapon known as Sudarshan Chakra was created.

[Again this story contradicts with the one that is given in the Bhagawata Purana about Sudarshan Chakra's origin].

Shiva declared: "I shall certainly fight with you. But first I wish to test your strength. Can you raise this Chakra with your big toe? shall condescend to enter into a duel with you only if you could lift the Chakra with your big toe."

Jalandhara tried to do this with his full strength. But no mater how hard be tried he failed to succeed. At last, with a great deal of difficulty, he managed to raise the Chakra and place it on his shoulders. But as soon as he did this, the weapon sliced off his head. The whole universe was cluttered up with Jalandhara's flesh and blood. Shiva made his henchpersons carry this mess to Yama, the god of death. It was with Jalandhara's flesh and blood that Yama created a hell called Maharaurava. This is how Jalandhara was slain by Shiva whose incinerating gaze was enough to burn all the companions of Jalandhara to ashes.

[This story is at sharp variance from the one given in the 'Shiva-Purana' which appears more authentic and meaningful. In order to help the curious reader realise the basic idea behind Jalandhar's story, the other version is also being quoted below].

Another Version of Jalandhara's Tale

Once Indra went to have the 'Darshan' of Lord Shiva at Mount Kailash. He was also accompanied by the divine priest Brihaspati. When Lord Shiva learnt about their arrival, in order to test the firmness of faith the visitors displayed, he adopted the guise of an old bearded ascetic and stationed himself at the gate of his Kailash abode. Coming near when Indra asked the old ascetic about Lord Shiva, he kept mum—pretending to have been lost in meditation. Drunk in the wine of his exalted position, the arrogant Indra thought as if the old ascetic was deliberately showing contempt to him. Enraged. Indra hit the quiet ascetic with his thunderbolt. But the mystic power of the ascetic (Shiva) blunted the edge of Indra's weapon. Indra's temerity made the ascetic's (Shiv's) Third Eye open and a fierce fire shot forth from it. Then Brihaspati recognised the ascetic's real identity and requested Shiva to forgive Indra. Though Shiva acceded to the request, the fire that emanated from Shiva's third eye could not be controlled. So Shiva took that fire, now in a beacon form, and threw it into the 'Ksheera Sagar' (ocean of milk) where it emerged in the form of a radiant and powerful boy. The new-born boy began to wail loudly at the shore of the ocean, causing distress even to the Guardians of the Quarters who informed Brahma, the Creator. The Creator reached near the boy and took him into his lap. But that boy put his arms round Brahma and suppressed the Creator's throat so powerfully that the aged Lord Brahma had tears welling up in his eyes. Seeing the boy's great power, the creator gave him the name 'Jalandhara' ('he who carries water'). Then the Creator looked at the boy's future and predicted him to be becoming the master of the demon race. "He shall be invincible to all except Lord Shiva who would eventually cause his end."

The Creator also advised the ocean to rear the boy up. When that boy, Jalandhara came of age he was married to demon Kalinemi's beautiful daughter named Vrinda. Seeing Jalandhara's incomparable might the demon chief Shukracharya appointed him the king of all demon-race. Shukracharya also told him as to how Vishnu, by his cunningness, had duped the demons of their legimitate right over the gems that were churned out of the ocean. Hearing this, Jalandhara sent a messenger to the chief of gods, Indra, with the threat: "either return the gems or face war". But Indra treated that messenger with utter contempt. When he returned, the messenger told Indra the sorry treatment meted out to him. This made Jalandhar attack the gods with his billion-strong demon army. Supported by the demon-commanders, Shumba and Nishumba, the demons attacked the gods. Although both the sides had innumerable casualties, the demons were revived to life again by Shukracharya who knew the Sanjivani 'idya.

Meanwhile, the divine priest also got hold of the Sanjivani Booty' (life-reviving herb) from the 'Drona-giri' (the Drona-mount). Seeing the gods also revived Shukracharya advised the demon-lord to uproot the mount Drona and throw deep into the ocean. The demon-lord, Jalandhara, did so and the divine forces started losing. Then the divine priest advised Indra to cease fighting as they were sure to lose. The gods fled and Jalandhara established his hold, without any trouble on the divine capital, Amaravati.

When the defeated gods reassembled in a secret Himalayan cave and brooded on their course of action, they decided to seek help from Lord Vishnu to get back their lost empire. Lord Vishnu was ready, as ever, to help the gods. But when his consort Lakshmi heard about the gods' scheme, she requested her Lord not to kill Jalandhara as he was her brother—both being born from the ocean. Vishnu acceded to her request and befriended the Demon, to the great chagrin of the gods. The gods then sought the scheming sage Narada's advice who said: "Not until this demon antagonises Lord Shiva that he could be slained." Then on the gods' request he devised a scheme and went to meet Jalandhar. The demon lord welcomed the divine sage Narada in his realm and showed him great respect. Narada then told him: "O Demon Lord! I have come here straight from the realm of Lord Shiva which extends to 10,000 yojanas. There you have the best that life can offer you. While roaming there I was told that even your realm matches well with the realm of Shiva. It was to confirm this contention that I came here to visit your kingdom. No doubt that you have everything that Lord Shiva has, but you lack in one thing. Lord Shiva has a gem of woman as his consort who is incomparable. If you can get hold of that gem, you may make your realm perfect."

Narada succeeded in kindling Jalandhar's lust for Lord Shiva's that 'incomparable' spouse and he dispatched his messenger, to Kailash mount, with the express demand that Parvati, the consort of Lord Shiva, be forthwith sent to his realm. Lord Shiva was furious to learn about this outrageous demand. His anger produced a terrible being called 'Barbar' who went to Jalandhar and warned him of dire consequence should he not go to Lord Shiva to apologise for his outrageous demand. But Narada had bloated Jalandhara's ego and the demon lord decided to take on Lord Shiva's forces. Soon a fierce battle took place in which the demons had to flee before the terrible might of the henchmen of Lord Shiva. Seeing his forces depleted the demon decided to wage an illusive war. He quickly disguised himself as Lord Shiva and reached before Parvati to abduct her. But seeing the exquisite beauty of the goddess he ejaculated and was exposed. Parvati hid herself in a secret cave.

Meanwhile, when Shiva learnt about Jalandhar's heinous attempt, he consulted Vishnu, saying, "Why are you still siding with this immoral demon? Why don't you come out and help the gods?" Then Vishnu told Shiva the reason behind his siding with Jalandhara whom he thought to be his brother-in-law in a way. But when he heard about Jalandhara's villainous and deceitful attempt he decided to teach him a lesson. He said: 'This demon is deriving all powers because of his wife Vrinda's unswerving wifely devotion. Now since he has tried to dupe Goddess Parvati, we have every right to pay him back in the same coin."

And then on Shiva's advice, Vishnu repaired to the realm of Jalandhara and stayed there in a garden. Meanwhile, the devoted wife of the demon lord Jalandhara, Vrinda, dreamt that her husband, naked with oil smeared on his body, was heading due south. He also appeared clad only in the garlands of black flower, and was surrounded with dreadful beasts. When she woke up, she was quite disturbed and in an attempt to shake off that dreadful vision, went to the garden in the company of her friends. Then suddenly she found the whole of her garden covered with dreadful beings. Her friends fled in panic and Vrinda, terrified, went near that meditating ascetic who was none other than Vishnu in disguise. The ascetic let out a weird c y to shoo all the gods away and Vrinda, in her relief, put her hands round the neck of that ascetic. While she was there, she found two monkeys coming there with the head and the lower body of her lord, Jalandhara, who was presumably dead. Then she requested the ascetic to revive her dead husband to life and the ascetic said: "No one slain by Lord Shiva can be brought back to life. But since you have sought my shelter. I would request Lord Shiva to help me bring his body back to life."

He did so and Vrinda found her husband once again alive. Happily she surrendered herself to her husband's passion and they enjoyed the bliss in copulation for long.

But, in fact, that husband was not the real demon lord Jalandhara but an illusive creation of Vishnu. Thus Lord Vishnu, on the advice of Lord Shiva, could manage to sully the wifely devotion of Vrinda to her husband which sapped the power that Jalandhara enjoyed. When Vrinda learnt about the trick played by Vishnu, she cursed him: "In the Age of Treta you shall also be seperated from your wife who shall be abducted by a demon." But on Vishnu's request she modified her curse by saying that with the help of the monkeys he might get back her wife. Saying so, Vrinda immolated herself in the holy fire and her vital force's essence entered the body of Parvati, so far hiding in a cave, frightened of Jalandhara's amoral advances. When that vital force of Vrinda entered Parvati's body she came out again in the open, to the great delight of her husband, Lord Shiva, and the gods merrily welcomed her.

Getting his wife back, Lord Shiva renewed his attack on Jalandhara, now considerably weakened because of his wife's demise. But still, undaunted, the demon lord, raged a magic war, making an illusion as though Lord Shiva's consort, Parvati, was tied to his chariot's one wheel. Deeming her wife to be in that pathetic state, Lord Shiva assumed his dreadful Rudra form, and hacked off Jalandhara's head by his trident. The vital force that emerged from Jalandhara's body coalesced with the body of Lord Shankar. The gods, delighted at the extermination of their mighty enemy, sang ovations in the honour of Lord Shiva.

[It is mentioned in other Puranas that Vrinda, in her next life, took birth as the sacred plant Tulsi (basil) and her personalised form was the darling of Lord Krishna in the Dwapar Age. Modern Vrindavana was the place where this sacred plant emerged. Hence the name Vrindavana. Also Vrinda's curse came true in Vishnu's incarnation as Lord Rama in the Treta Age.]

[The whole episode appears to be an extended allegory. It appears that this sacred plant was the preserve of water

(Jalandhara) and the gods, realising the special medicinal qualities of basil, tried to make it grow on the land where this could be put to better use. All the tales connected with Vrinda point to this logical conclusion. In fact, most of the Hindu scriptures have the scientific facts so thinly woven in the form of fictional tales that it becomes difficult to separate the chaff from the real grain. This whole episode is a classical example of that attempt.]

The Slaying of the Demon Lord Andhaka

Clad in the tiger's skin with the serpents giving the impression of the sacred thread, Lord Shiva was seated on the mount Kailash, lost in meditation one day. He was surrounded by flowers and birds, animals and spirits—all radiant because of his patronising presence. Heavenly music filled the air, and the perfume of sandalwood rose to the nostril.

Enchanted by this peaceful scene Parvati came in a playful mood and going to her beloved husband she put her hands over his eyes. The effect was tremendous: the light in the universe went out—life began to fade and all living beings were full of fear. The sweat that oozed out of the hands of Parvati on touching Shiva became a physical being—a horrible black and blind boy. Parvati was baffled seeing that dreadful existence but Shiva said that since that boy came from their physical contact, he is verily Parvati's son. When Hiranyaksha, the elder brother of the demon Hiranyakashyapu[1], observed great austerities to propitiate Lord Shiva, the God appeared before him and gifted that boy as the reward of his penance. The boy was called Andhaka because of his blindness. After Hiranyaksha that Andhaka became the lord of the demons, although other members of the demon clan had misgivings because they considered him to be not real demon because he was a divine product.

This was the thorn that rankled Andhaka's heart. Disowned by the majority of his clan he repaired to the deep caves to meditate upon the holy visage of the Creator. Propitiated, Lord Brahma came before him and Andhaka requested him to make him invincible for the gods and the demons and that his whole clan should accept him as their Lord. Also, he requested that his eyes should also become

1. The celeberated demon lord, the father of Prahlad, who was killed by Vishnu's Narasimha Incarnation. Read ahead about him.

all right. Although Brahma granted the fulfilment of his all desires, the Creator warned that he was to be vanquished or killed by only Lord Shiva—for nothing in this world can face or survive before a wroth Shiva."

As soon as he returned to his capital he subdued all his opponents and began to rule merrily. Soon his might increased as much as to overwhelm even the gods. But due to his unbridled authority he soon developed arrogance. One day he asked his minister whether there was anyone in the world capable of matching his strength, majesty and riches. Whereupon his minister pointed out that he lacked the company of a beautiful woman. The most beautiful woman in the world, he said, was the pride possession of an ascetic with the matted hair, dwelling on the Mount Kailash. He indirectly hinted that he must strive to possess Parvati if he wanted to be matchless all over the world. By this time he had forgotten everything about his connection with Lord Shiva and the warning that he received from the Creator. So, provoked, he immediately dispatched the messenger to that ascetic (Lord Shiva) with the message that the most beautiful woman (Parvati) should be given to him. Shiva, on getting this outrageous demand showed it the contempt it deserved. When the messenger returned he not only gave the reaction of that 'matted man' to Andhaka but also a vivid description of Parvati whom he could see.

All this information fuelled the longing for the woman and the resolve to teach that ascetic a lesson. He immediately rushed to that cave where Shiva was engaged in perfecting his renowned weapon, the Pashupati Astra. Andhaka, flanked by all the choicest demon warriors came charging upon the cave. But Lord Shiva's henchpersons positioned to guard the cave quickly repulsed the demon's attack. Although the attackers made repeated attacks they remained unsuccessful. Since the attacks were disturbing Shiva's concentration, he left for some unknown destination.

One day, while the henchpersons of Shiva were away, Andhaka, charged with a lecherous desire, entered the cave and found Parvati alone. Parvati fought with Andhaka initially. But when she found Andhaka to be overwhelming, she mentally requested the gods to come to her help. They joined the fray and the battle raged for many years. But no decision could emerge finally from that confrontation. At last Shiva was told about the cause of the fight and he came to the fray, declaring temporary ceasefire. But the demon Andhaka was maddened by his desire to possess Parvati. Although peace efforts were repeatedly made, Andhaka would not relent. He again insisted that till he got 'that woman' no peace between the gods and demons was possible. At last the armed confrontation again ensued.

Andhaka renewed the assault keeping his trusted lieutenant, Bali, in the front. Bali fought so fiercely that he single-handedly defeated all the gods including Brahma, Vishnu, Indra and Surya. Not only this he spread his mouth far and wide to even swallow all the deities. Getting the news Shiva came rushing forward and hurled so powerful weapons as to force the demons to disgorge all the swallowed deities. In revenge Shankar (Lord Shiva) himself swallowed the demon priest, 'Shukracha ya'. The morale of the demons sagged and they were defeated. Once out of the demon's mouth, Indra again challenged him. Then Andhaka severely distressed Indra by his keen arrows. In order to save Indra, Lord Shiva began to cast massive blows on the demons by his heavy trident. But the blood of the demon that gushed out of his wounds created as many eerie demons as the drops of the blood that fell on to the ground. Then the gods invoked the fighting female spirit, Chandi who began to lick the blood of that demon. At last Shiva succeeded in hacking the demon Andhaka's head off. But since the demon had chanted Shiva's name before dying, Lord Shiva granted the soul of Andhaka asylum in his realm.

Although the demon had been slayed, the demon priest, Shukracharya, was still inside the stomach of Lord Shiva. Despite Shukracharya's attempt to find a suitable opening to come out, he failed. At last, getting desperate, he began to chant the following Shloka for his release:

OM NAMASTE DEVE SHAYA SURAASUR NAMASKRITAAYA, BHOOT-BHAVYA MAHADEVAAYA HARIT-PINGALALOCHANAAYA

[I bow to the Lord of the gods ever adored by the demons and the gods alike. The Lord, who casts the being's destiny, (may help me) who has greenish yellow eyes].

This was the Mantra Shiva himself had taught to Shukracha ya once. By the efficacy of the mantra, Shiva allowed Shukracharya to come out through the Lord's phallus. [Since then semen has begun to be called Shukra]. Coming out, the grateful Shukra bowed before Lord Shiva who out of his grace also revealed to Shukra the 'Mrita-Sanjeevani Vidya' (the art of reviving the dead).

The Slaying of the Demons Hiranyaksha and Hiranyakashyapu

While reciting the Purana, the Sootaji said: "Once the earth was taken to the Rasatala (lowest level) by the demon-lord Hiranyaksha. It was retrieved to its normal level by Vishnu when he incarnated as the Boar." Whereupon Lomaharshana (Sootaji) recounted the following tale.

As has already been mentioned the demon mother Diti had two prominent sons. Their names were Hirankyaksha and Hiranyakashyapu. Hiranyaksha (the golden eyed) was a very powerful demon. He had won a boon from Brahma through spending many ages in austerities.

[It should be noted that even Brahma cannot prevent the attainment of powers won through determined efforts; it is the use to which these powers are put which makes them good or bad. It is only when they are put to evil purposes that the culprit is destroyed by either Vishnu or Shiva. Brahma, the Creator, had no concern as to how his creatures behaved. It was always the other two super-deities that came to destroy that evil creature].

The boon was that he should become king of the whole world, and that no animal which he mentioned by name should have the power to harm him. In his catalogue of animals he forgot to name the boar. When in his arrogance he had dragged the earth down into the ocean it complained to the gods. They all first went to Brahma who said: "It is not me but Vishnu who can redeem the earth." Whereupon all, led by the earth in the form of a cow, reached Vishnu's Loka (Vaikuntha). Reassuring them, Vishnu adopted the form of a Varaha (boar) whose name Hiranyaksha had failed to include. Vishnu, therefore, took the form of a boar[1], with

1. In fact the whole series of incarnations of Lord Vishnu reminds one about the theory of evolution. He took the form of a Fish when it was all water. Then he took the form of a Boar when it was wet and partially covered with water. It is at this stage the earth gets covered with filth caused by the decomposition of the

great white tusks, and plunged into the ocean to free the earth. It took him a thousand years to kill Hiranyaksha and lift the earth with his tusks to the proper level.[2] Concluding the story of Hiranyaksha, the Sootaji, beholding the curiosity of the sages, started reciting the story of Hiranyakashyapu.

Hiranyakashyapu had replaced his brother, Hiranyaksha, as the demon lord. He had observed great austerities also and received boon from the Creator Brahma of his almost invincibility. When Hiranyakashyapu started to rule as the demon lord, he had become very powerful. The boon that he received from Brahma had allowed him to be unslayable by any man or god or a beast, neither in the daytime nor at night and neither inside any premises nor out of it, nor on the land or in water. His boon from Brahma made him almost invincible. He conquered the three worlds and driving out Indra from heaven he assumed himself the lordship of even the divinities. He also assumed the titles of Savita, Vayu, Agni, Varuna, Kubera and Yama. He routed the gods out of heaven who roamed about here and there shelterless. He was now the sole authority of the universe. Everyone had to worship him only. He was now the master of all creations. He dwelled in a magnificent palace made of crystals.

He had four sons but his third son, Prahlad, was a precocious child. That boy learnt his lessons fast and while studying the scriptures he developed intense devotion for Vishnu. Once Hiranyakashyapu asked him: "What have you learnt so far?"

---

natural product. The boar is the animal which eats this filth as we still see it doing. Hence the Boar Incarnation. Then comes the incarnation of Narasimha or man-lion. It is only in the 7th incarnation of Lord Rama that this being could evolve itself to exalted manhood. Rama was the complete man who is repeatedly referred to as man par excellence. Lord Krishna represents the total growth of human intelligence having both the shades of moral and immoral aspects of life.

2. In one of the versions of this Purana it is decribed that the earth earned the epithat 'Prithivi' only after this Boar incarnation. 'Prithvi' literally means the extended one, with the view of the earth growing out of water.

"I have learnt to pray Vishnu, the great Lord", Prahlad replied.

Hiranyakashyapu was quite enraged listening to this reply. Vishnu was an anathema. Thereafter, no matter what way he tried to punish Prahlad he couldn't efface that devotion to Vishnu from his son's heart. At last Hiranyakashyapu was slayed by Vishnu assuming the famous Narasimha (man-lion) form[1].

[The Linga Purana introduces a further twist in the story, in an obvious attempt to glorify Lord Shiva.]

However, after killing Hiranyakashyapu, Lord Vishnu did not give up his 'man-lion' form. The being raged everywhere in the universe, threatening to destroy the whole creation.

The gods, led by Brahma, fled to Shiva on Mount Kailash. They requested: "Please save us from the scourge of this lion".

Shiva assured the gods that he would take care of 'Narasimha'.

Then Lord Shiva created a being known as Veerabhadra from his own body. Veerabhadra was another manifestation of Lord Shiva himself. That strange being, Veerabhadra, had three eyes and he held several weapons in his hand. His teeth were as sharp as the crescent moon, his eyebrows were like rainbows and his beard was as dark as the clouds.

"What have you created me for?" asked Veerabhadra.

"A being named Narasimha is causing havoc", replied Shiva. "It is Vishnu who had adopted this form. The universe must be rid of this being 'Narasimha'. First try to persuade him to give up this form. If that attempt fails, kill him."

Getting this instruction, Veerabhadra straightaway went to Narasimha (Vishnu) and told him: "Vishnu! You are the preserver of the universe. There are several occasions when you have adopted incarnations so as to save the world. Why have you adopted this 'Narasimha' form? Please give it up at once. Your this form seems to be threatening the world with its eventual extinction."

These words merely went on to further fuel the anger of that charged man-lion. He roared: "I don't need any advice

1. For getting the details of this story of Hiranyakashyapu please read the 'Vishnu Purana' of our Purana series.

from you". He said, "Return to whence you came. I will destroy the universe. Who are you to decree otherwise? I am the lord of everything. Brahma, the Creator, is my product. Hence you, in the fear of your own existence, must have me in peace. I am the Master of Universe and I would act as I deem fit."

"But you appear to have forgotten about Lord Shiva," said Veerbhadra. "Don't forget that Lord Shiva is the Lord Supreme. He is the final authority and the Destroyer of the Universe. And if you do not come to your senses, he is going to destroy you as well. Be forewarned. I am Veerabhadra. Have you forgotten what havoc had I wrought in the Yagya of Daksha?"

These words further angered Vishnu. He was as much provoked as to attack Veerabhadra who had adopted a strange form that was half-deer and half-bird. It had a thousand arms and the crescent moon shone on its head. The wings were huge with sparks issued out of his eyes. Its claws were exceedingly sharp. Veerabhadra grasped Vishnu and rose up into the sky. He flung Vishnu down repeatedly on the ground and picked him up again.

This thrashing brought the arrogant Vishnu back to his senses and he started to pray Shiva. He called upon Shiva by his 1000 names.

But Veerabhadra killed Vishnu's that incarnation. He sliced off Narasimha's head and skinned the pelt. "This, however, doesn't mean", explained the Sootaji, "that Vishnu died. It was only his incarnatin that was finished off. Vishnu merged into Shiva. Narasimha's pelt is worn by Shiva as clothing. And the skulls that Shiva wears as his ornaments round his neck contain one skull of Narasimha."

The Story of Upamanyu

There was a boy named Upamanyu who was once taken on a visit to his maternal uncle's house. His maternal uncle was in a better financial condition. But ironically when milk was given to him to drink, that was a little diluted than what his cousins were offered. So he asked his mother: "Why can't I have better milk to drink?" His mother started to weep. "My son!" she said, "We are poor. We do not have the money to buy you good milk". But so insistent was her son that the mother ground some rice with water and gave it to her son to drink, pretending that it was milk. As soon as his mother gave him that concoction, he tasted it and realised it was not milk at all. With the result, discerning through his mother's deceitful trick he started crying even more profusely. At last his mother told him: "Please do not cry. Unfortunately we are poor. The only option left for those who suffer from misfortune is to pray Shiva. Perhaps we are amiss in that we did not pray Shiva is our earlier lives. In order to get rid of one's distress one must pray to Shiva."

Thus instructed Upamanyu started to meditate. He built for himself a hermitage in the Himalayas.

Beholding him to be so determinedly worshipping him, Lord Shiva decided to test Upamanyu. He appeared before the boy in the guise of Indra and said: "I am pleased with your 'Tapasya' and will grant you a boon. What boon do you wish for?"

Upamanyu was rather surprised. He wanted to propitiate not Indra but Shiva. But he said with great reverence, "I am indeed fortunate that the king of the gods has come to visit me," replied Upamanyu. "Please grant me the boon that I may be devoted to Shiva."

"Who is Shiva? That naked ascetic having the serpents as his ornaments", that pseudo Indra (Shiva) said disdanifully. "I am the king of the gods. I am much superior to him. You should worship me instead."

Upamanyu was wroth at such a disdainful reference to his chosen lord Shiva by that fake Indra. He thought that he had committed a great sin in allowing such insults to be uttered in his presence. He decided to kill himself as he could hear such profane words referred to his chosen lord. As he was about to hurl himself down from the hill he was meditating, Shiva appeared before Upamanyu in his true form and blessed the boy. Owing to Lord Shiva's grace Upamanyu never suffered the lack of milk to drink.

[According to this Purana, subsequently it was this Upamanyu who taught Pashupata Vrata to Lord Krishna. The same Upamanyu also figures in the Mahabharata wherein he, too, shows his preference for milk].

Sati or Shakti, the First Wife of Lord Shiva

One of the daughters of Daksha-Prajapati was Shakti (or Sati). Daksha was at first unwilling to give his daughter Sati in marriage to Shiva whom he despised because of his queer way of living. But since Sati developed love for Shiva owing to the divine inkling, Daksha was persuaded by Brahma to accept him as the bridegroom. Besides Shiva's queer way of living, Daksha also carried an ill-will for Shiva owing to another reason. Once in the court of Brahma, Shiva had not respectfully greeted Daksha and kept sitting while all the gods and sages had shown due regard. Since Shiva was married to his daughter, he felt it quite badly.

Nevertheles, after marriage Shiva was living with Sati happily at the Kailash mount (the eternal abode of Shiva). Once when Sati saw Shiva bowing to Rama (the incarnation of Lord Vishnu) she developed some misgivings because she thought her lord to have been superior to Vishnu. Although Shiva explained that Rama was the mortal manifestation of Lord Vishnu, Sati was not convinced. Then Shiva asked her to judge herself whether Rama was just a mortal being or a divine incarnation. Sati had seen Rama distressed in separation from Sita. So she thought if she could adopt Sita's form and reach before Rama she would know whether Rama was a divine incarnation or not. For a mortal being was likely to be duped seeing Sita before but a divine incarnation would know her to be not the real Sita. But as she reached before Rama and Lakshman, though Lakshman was taken aback but Rama immediately recognised her to be spouse of Lord Shiva. Sati returned having confirmed that Rama was the divine incarnation.

Meanwhile, Shiva realised through his psychic powers all that had taken place. So when Sati returend he asked her to sit in front and not at his left side which was her normal position as the wife. Later on she realised that Shiva had done so because she had adopted Sita's form who was motherly to him. As such he couldn't have accepted her any more as his wife. Now Shiva's mentally deserting her as wife was a great blow to Sati. After all, she had done so at his bidding. But Shiva's decision was immutable. She had to put up with this situation. It was only then that she learned about her father Daksha's arranging a Yagya at a large scale. But her father had not invited her or her husband to it owing to the grudge he carried for Shiva. However, despite Shiva's objection to her going there uninvited, she insisted and reached the venue of the Yagya. She was neglected there by all save her mother. However, when she found her husband receiving no share in the Yagya offering despite being such an exalted god, due to her father's prejudice, she decided to end her life by self-immolating her to death by jumping into the holy fire.

Sati's ending her life through the holy fire disturbed the proceedings of the Yagya severely. The assistant of Lord Shiva, Nandi, who had escorted Sati to the venue, returned quickly to apprise Shiva about the death of Sati and her reasons for committing suicide. When Shiva heard of this he rose in great anger and, plucking from his head a lock of hair, flung it to the ground. It became transformed into a dreadful being called Veerabhadra—terrible to look at, with three flaming eyes and a thousand arms, wearing a garland of skulls and carrying a number of weapons. Shiva appointed him the leader of his terrible army comprising even ghosts, goblins and hounds. He then told Veerabhadra to destroy Daksha and his Yagya as well. Veerabhadra, creating more of his soldiers from the pores of his skin, went to Daksha's yagya, broke the holy vessels, insulted the priests, broke Yama's staff, trod on Indra and hacked off Daksha's head. Bhrigu the high sage and the priest of the Yagya had his one eye pierced. The gods fled in terror.

By then, Shiva also reached there to search for the body of his dead wife and when he found it, he picked it up reverentially, placed across his shoulders and walked from the venue. Seven times round the world he went with his burden, so majestic in his wrath and in the depth of his grief that all beings were terrified. The earth trembled in fear, the soil lost its moisture, the plants died and famine came. At last all the people and the gods prayed Vishnu to provide the succour. He realised that Shiva won't be ormal till that dead body was destroyed. So he repeatedly hurled his Sudarshan Chakra to cut that body into pieces and relieve Shiva of the dead burden. Sati's dead body was cut into twelve pieces which fell to the ground. The spot where each piece fell emerged as the 'Shakti-Patha' (the seat of the Goddess Sati). After this Shiva became normal and the earth heaved a sigh of relief. However, Shiva's first marriage ended in a disaster.

Uma or Parvati, Shiva's Second Wife

The gods who had been routed at Daksha's sacrifice went to Brahma for advice and he told them to make peace with Shiva. He himself went with them and they found Shiva in meditation. Brahma approached him and asked him to forgive Daksha and make good all the damage that had been done to gods and men for, he pointed out, all the sacrificial offerings belonged to him (Shiva) in reality and he should, therefore, allow them to be completed. Shiva agreed and all became as before. One difficulty arose for Daksha's head had been lost in the tumult! However, Shiva found a goat's head nearby and placed it on Daksha's shoulders—thus making true what Nanda had said as he left Daksha's court when Sati died: "If you, Daksha, live after committing this sacrilege, it can only be with a goat's head instead of a human head!" When the sacrifice was completed Vishnu himself, riding on Garuda, came at its valedictory function and told Daksha that he (Vishnu), Shiva and Brahma were all one.

Sati, before dying, had prayed the Holy Fire, to make her Shiva's wife in next life also. Her wish was fulfilled and Sati took her next birth as the daughter of the great Himavant (the ruler of the Himalayan range) and got the name Uma or Girija or Parvati. In this new birth she continued to worship Shiva, often escaping from her home during the night to place flowers and burn lights at his shrine.

Immediately after her birth, Narada happened to reach Himavant's palace and the curious father requested the divine sage to foretell about his daughter's future—as was the custom those days. When Narada saw the tiny girl's palm and her horoscope, he declared: "She is a divine being and shall be renowned as the ideal wife. Her husband will be immortal, so she will be in his company. Both of them will form the Eternal Pair. But there is one bad thing about her husband. He will be fatherless, a wandering ascetic, uncouth, reveller with horrible form and with reprehensible company." When the parents of the girl expressed their shock and dismay, allaying their apprehensions Narada said: "Don't worry. All these negative points will become virtue in Shiva's case who shall be her husband."

This prognostication made Parvati love Shiva right since her childhood. She developed natural love for Shiva—perhaps due to her previous life's memories. She used to fight with anyone deriding her chosen lord in comparison to other gods like Vishnu or Indra.

Shiva was unaware of these tidings as he was still deeply lost in meditation. About this time the gods were in great panic owing to that dreadful demon Taraka. Brahma had told that it was only Shiva's son who could destroy this demon. But for that Shiva must marry. But the great lord had become indifferent to every worldly pleasure, being all the time lost in meditation.

As Shiva was not even approachable, Indra, the chief of the gods, went to the lord of love, Kaam and sought his help. Kaam took his companion Vasant (spring season) and attempted to rouse in Shiva an amorous mood. But a wroth Shiva opened his third eye to make that lord of love instantly burnt to ashes. When Rati, the wife of Kaam, requested, Shiva said that in Dwapar her husband would get back his body and during the interregnum he would survive as only an emotion sans body. This happened when Lord Krishna's son Pradyumna took birth in the Dwapar Yuga.

Meanwhile, Uma also learnt about Shiva's indifference to marrying again. But she was determined to marry him only. In order to do rigorous penance to get him as her husband, she took off her beautiful clothes and jewels and wearing the hermit's dress left for the jungles.

The gods, in the meanwhile, were greatly worried and they sent a delegation to the high sages to impress upon Lord Shiva that his marrying was necessary not only for the gods' survival but for the whole world because the demon was making the entire system of the earth go topsy-turvy. At last, Shiva agreed but said that he would like Uma's faith in him to be tested first. The gods' arranged a delegation of the seers for this purpose.

One day Uma was picking flowers for her regular worship when some young Brahmanas visited her. They asked as to why she, who was so young and fair, was spending his time this way. Then she told them about her story. Whereupon they tried to warn her about Shiva: a horrible character, who visited the burning grounds with poisonous snakes coiled round his neck and the ghosts and goblins to give him company. Hearing this, instead of turning herself against Shiva, Uma grew ang y on the Brahmanas. She said she would not listen to their deprication against Shiva but would continue to be devoted to her chosen lord. When the group of Brahmanas returned to tell Shiva about Uma's unflinching love and devotion to him, Shiva agreed to marry her.

Flanked by Brahma and Vishnu and accompanied by all the gods, mortals, demons, goblins ghosts and spirits, Shiva reached the marriage canopy on the appointed day and the ceremony was performed amidst much merriment and jest. During the ceremony, the bride's mother, Maina, was 'shooed' away by the snakes in a light banter when she came to perform the 'Aarti' round the bridegroom's face. After staying with Himavant for a month, Shiva and Parvati, the eternal couple, left for Kailash. At due time they had their first son, called Kartikeya.

Shiva and Uma's Sons: Kartikeya and Ganesh

Kartikeya—After Lord Shiva's marriage with Uma, the gods were eagerly waiting for the birth of their son. At last Lord Agni (Agni-deva) was sent to Kailash to remind Shiva about his promise to the gods. Shiva gave his seed which the fire-god swallowed, adopting the form of a pigeon. But the seed was so hot that even the fire-god failed to carry. Then Shiva advised him to have his seed placed in the womb of some woman. Brahma also advised Agni to have his bath in the holy Sangam at Prayagraj (modern Allahabad). At Prayagraj Agni had Shiva's seed planted in the womb of the six wives of the holy sages called Krittikas through their pores of the skin. All those six women became pregnant and their husbands deserted them for adultery. With the result they all began to dwell at the Himalayas. At due time they all delivered and each of them threw the foetus in the river Ganga. Even the cool Ganga could not bear their combined form and threw the foetuses on the forest of the reeds. There on the sixth day of the bright half of the lunar month Margasheersha came into existence, the son of Shiva. Since he was the product of the six Krittikas, he had six faces and named Kartikeya (literally, of Krittikas). [Because of his six faces he is also called Shadaanana. His other names are Skanda and Subramanyam]. Soon the news of his birth spread all over the world, to the great delight of the gods.

All this while Shiva was unaware of these happenings. Once Uma asked him about his seed he had given to Agni. "Has it been wasted?" she asked. Then Shiva made enquiry and learnt about the birth of Kartikeya or Shadaanana. The eternal pair immediately repaired to the mount the child was dwelling at, fostered by the divine female existences called Krittikas. Then taking along their son the eternal couple reached back Kailash. Uma was sorry to have been deprived of the happiness of becoming a mother—producing the child from her own womb. When she learnt about the gods' scheme to get the seed of Shiva, she cursed all the divine ladies that they shall ever remain incapable of producing any child.

Kartikeya, in due time grew up to be a young person. Indra and other gods then approached Shiva, asking if Kartikeya could now fight Tarakasura. Shiv agreed and appointed Kartikeya the commander of the divine forces. He was presented with the choicest divine weapons by various gods. While going to Indra's capital, Amaravati, he saw the damage which Taraka had done and became very ang y and anxious to fight the demon. Preparations began for the battle. The gods rode on their vehicles: Kartikeya on a peacock, which he chose as his favourite mount, Indra came on his elephant Airavata, Agni on ram, Yama on a buffalo and Varuna on a dolphin. The strange array struck terror into Tarakasura's army and his soldiers began to panic. The battle eventually turned into a duel between Taraka and Kartikeya. Although the demon resorted to even a magic war, Kartikeya neutralised all his attacks and finally plunged his lance into him and killed him instantly. After killing the demon Taraka, Kartikeya's fame spread far and wide. He killed the demon Banasura also and made his abode at the Kraunch Parvata (the heron-shaped mount, in south).

Kartikeya is also known as Skanda. When he was just a boy Indra had unknowingly fought with him. It is said when Indra hurled his thunderbolt on the left, right and centre of Kartikeya's body, three persons emerged from his three wounds. Their names are Shakti, Vishakh and Nigam. Aided by these three when Kartikeya again challenged Indra, he ran away and later the chief of the gods had to apologise. Since then these four persons—verily one person's parts—came to be combinedly known as Skanda.

Ganesh—According to this Purana Ganesh was born when Lord Shiva was absent from Kailash. The Purana says that he was born of the scurf of Parvati's body. When he grew up Parvati asked him to guard her palace and allow no entry until she permitted. Once Parvati was taking bath when Lord Shiva happened to return to Kailash from his abode in Varanasi. The boy standing guard at Parvati's chamber refused to let Shiva go in. Neither Shiva nor Ganesh knew each other. When objected to allow him entry into his wife's chamber, Shiv . was furious. And then a scuffle ensued and the boy defeated all the supporters of Lord Shiva single-handed. At last Lord Shiva himself came to fight and hacked off the recalcitrant boy's head. All this while Parvati was inside, taking her bath. When she heard the war cries, she came out only to find her beloved son beheaded. Enraged she was about to curse all the gods but Shiva tried to placate her and said the boy, though headless, was not dead. He immediately promised to bring him back to life if only the head of any other being could be procured pronto. The only condition was that the being ought to have been born on the same day and time when Ganesh was born. Then Vishnu flew away on his mount Garuda to a forest in the north where, on the bank of a river, he saw a king elephant asleep. Having found that the elephant was exactly of Ganesh's age, he cut off its head with his Chakra (Sudarshana) and returned to Kailash with the elephant which he placed on that headless boy. Then, in order to make happy the ang y mother Parvati, all the gods promised that in every auspicious worship or ceremony, her son Ganesh shall always be the first god (deity) to be worshipped—even before the Surpeme Deity (Brahmana). With the boy coming back to life the Eternal Couple were delighted and all the gods blessed the boy Ganesh. While Vishnu gave him the blessing of knowledge, Brahma of fame and worship, Dharmaraja of righteousness and mercy, Shiva of generosity, intelligence, peace and self control, Lakshmi promised to live always where Ganesh is worshipped, Sarasvati granted him the power of speech and poetry, of memory and eloquence, Savitri—Brahma's wife—of all wisdom. And Ganesh began to dwell happily with his parents at Kailash.

When both the boys grew up, Shiva and Parvati thought of marrying them. While Kartikeya was the elder, Ganesh looked more mature. The parents called the boys together and told them that, as they loved them equally, they couldn't decide as to who should be the first to be married. Then it was decided that the one who would move around the world fastest would be the first to be married.

Although Ganesh agreed to this condition, he knew that

owing to his massive physique and the poor mouse as the vehicle, he might not succeed. But as he was more intelligent. He hit upon a brilliant solution. While Kartikeya rode upon his vehicle, the peacock, and went away to make a full round of the world. Ganesh took the ceremonial bath and asked his parents to sit on their thrones while he worshipped them. On being reminded about the contest by his parents Ganesh answered that he had already moved round the world as the scriptures claimed that moving around the parents was tantamount to having pilgrimage round the earth. His parents found his son's (Ganesh's) argument to be quite convincing and they quickly arranged for Ganesh's marriage to Riddhi and Siddhi—the daughters of Prajapati. All the gods came to attend the marriage ceremony which was solemnised under the guidance of Vishwakarma, the architect of the world. In due time Ganesh had two sons: Labha from his wife Riddhi and Kshem from his wife Siddhi. When Kartikeya learnt about Ganesh's marriage, he became very sad and under protest retired to the Kraunch Parvat in deep south. The Purana says that in order to make their son Kartikeya happy, Shiva visits him in south on the day of the new moon and Parvati on the full moon day.

Other popular names of Ganesh are Ganaadhipati, Umaputra, Heramba (the favourite of the mother), Gajaanana, Ekadanta, (one-tusked), Lambodara (with a long belly), Kumar-Bhrata (Kartikeya's brother) and Vinaayaka (special leader).

While Kartikeya is the commander-in-chief of the divine forces, Ganesh is the guardian of scribes. Since Ganesh ensures auspiciousness of any occasion be is also called Varadamoorti or Mangalamoorti.

Worship of the Lingam

Lingam is the symbol of Shiva. Lord Shiva is the easily propitiable deity. He is Ashutosh[1] (the deity who quickly satisfies his devotee by fulfilling his desire) and doesn't need an elaborate ritual for his gratification. Even the wild products like the fruit of Bel (wood apple or Aegle Mammelos), flowers of Aak (a wild shrub), the fruits of Ber (plums) etc., if given in the offering can satisfy this Lord. Not only this, just pouring of water or milk over his Lingam is enough to propitiate Lord Shiva.

Domestic worship is also offered to him. First of all the house-owner should ritually worship Lord Ganesh, Goddess Saraswati, followed by the ceremonial welcome of the priest. Then the Shodashopachara Poojan (worship through all the sixteen modes) should be undertaken. Now the place where the worshipper wishes to start the worship should be purified by reciting a 'Mantra' to propitiate the Mother Earth. Now a clay image of Shiva in the form of a Lingam should be prepared. After the 'Lingam' is ready the full ritual of the ceremony of animation should be completed. This process in Sanskrit is called Pran-Pratishthapan. It is through this process the Lingam is energised and it no more remains the material it has been devised from. This rite of animation is undertaken to consecrate the idol or the Lingam. The Lingam, having thus been made and consecrated, is solemnly placed on an unborn Bilva leaf and the 'puja' or worship is offered to it.

The temple worship is more elaborate. The worshipper begins the ceremony by 'Parikrama' (circumambulation) of the temple court seven times, always remembering to keep his right hand towards the shrine. He (the worshipper) then enters the vestibule or porch of the innermost shrine where the image is kept, and into which only the priest ('Pujari') is allowed to go. Generally there is suspended

1. Aashutosh literally means easily propitiable. But Shiva is also the one who quickly grants boon.

from the roof of the vestibule a bell which the worshipper strikes in order to arouse the attention of the Lord. The priest often blows—at fixed times—a conch-shell kept for the same purpose. The worshipper then advances to the threshold of the shrine and presents his offerings to the idol (Lingam)—like flowers, milk, fruits etc.) placed right at the sanctum sanctorum. Uttering a short verse or prayer begging the Lord's acceptance of his worship, accompanied with the act of prostration, or simply joining hands or lifting the hand to the forehead are necessary obligations to this act of worship. [This style of worship is more an attempt to establish the communion with the chosen Lord.]

The favourite time of worshipping Lord Shiva is Pradosha (the onset of the night) Kala (time) and his favourite day is Monday. The linking period between the thirteenth and the fourteenth day of the dark fortnight is believed to be the most favourite time to propitiate Lord Shiva during a month. All these celebrations and worship etc. become very significant during the Mahashivaratri time. This falls on Phalguna-Krishna Chaturdashi (fourteenth lunar date during the dark fortnight of the month Phalguna, which according to the English calendar is between 15th Feb. and 15th March). If Mahashivaratri falls on a Monday (Somavara) it is considered very auspicious. Somavara is the day of Lord Shiva. Soma means the Moon. The crescent moon is an adornment on Lord Shiva's matted hair. Because of this, Lord Shiva is also called 'Chandramauleeshwara' or 'Induchooda' as both Chandra and Indu mean the moon. The moon was given refuge by Lord Shiva is his matted hair when the luminary was under a curse. Because of this reason, people observe Somavara Vrata or fasting on Monday to please Lord Shiva.

If Mahashivaratri falls on Monday and also under the asterism of Ardra (ORIONIS) the day becomes doubly auspicious. On this special day, under Ardra, Lord Shiva becomes particularly merciful towards his devotees.

The Purana highlights the importance of this day by recounting a story which is given below. There lived a hunter in the Himalayan region many aeons ago. One day while he was hunting he was overtaken by nightfall. As he was anxious not to become a prey to the wild beasts, he climbed a tree. Tormented by cold and hunger he passed a miserable night is strict watchfulness. That night happened to be the Mahashivaratri day falling on Monday under the asterism of Ardra. And at the foot of the tree the hunter was taking refuge was a Lingam. That tree itself was a Bilwa tree. His discomforts obliged him to change his position frequently and the shaking of the tree caused some leaves of the Bilwa tree fall on the Lingam. When a few days after the hunter died, the messenger of the death-god, Yamadoota, happened to reach there to capture his soul. But they were prevented by Shiva's ganas who came to escort the hunter's soul to the realm of Lord Shiva on account of the hunter observing the fast on the Mahashivaratri Day and casting the Bilwapatra on the Lingam albeit accidentally. This led to a scuffle between the messengers of the death-god and Shiva. Eventually the messengers of Shiva succeeded in taking possession of the hunter's soul and in taking it to the realm of Lord Shiva. When Yama complained to Nandi of this treatment by Shiva's hench-persons, Nandi replied: "This man has been a great sinner who has not scrupled to shed blood, but before he died, he fasted, watched and offered the Bilwa leaves to the Lingam. This single action has cleansed him from his sins." During the four parts of Mahashivaratri night, one has to keep vigil and worship Shiva. At midnight, on the 'Chaturdarshi' (i.e., on 14th lunar tithi night), all holy waters and 'devatas' are said to merge in the Shivalingam.

Mythologically, it was on this sacred day Lord Shiva manifested himself as a Pillar of Light whose beginning or end could not be ascertained by the two super gods (Brahma and Vishnu)—meaning thereby that Lord Shiva's influence is unfathomable and that a Shivalingam is only a convenient, concrete form of all-pervading Lord for the devotees to offer worship. On Mahashivaratri day, both Brahma and Vishnu worshipped Shiva, setting an example to others that the day is particularly auspicious for invoking the blessings of Shiva. Those who fast day and night on Mahashivaratri day and worship the Shivalingam with Bilwa leaves will attain closeness to Shiva. All men and women should observe this fast for their welfare in this world and the next. The Purana says that those who observe this

'Vrata' for 12 years or more will become a 'Gana' (an attendant) of Lord Shiva.

The Purana says that once Parvati herself asked Shiva: "What are the disciplines to be observed on that day and night?" Lord Shiva replied: "One should maintain silence or one should not utter bad words. Singing hymns is of special significance on this day. One should bathe and then worship me with a pure heart and mind. Keeping ready all 'pooja' articles including the Bilwa leaves, flowers, fruits and Panchamrita [A special concoction prepared by mixing Milk, Curds, Honey, Sugar and Ghee with the sprinkling of the sacred Tulsi (basil) leaves], one should pray to me: "O Lord Shiva, please accept these offerings along with your spouse, Parvati". After this the devotee should do 'achamana' (rinsing ritually) thrice as a purificatory rite, and then do the 'Pranayam' (rhythmic breathing) to keep his attention pin-pointed. Then one should repeat the 'Panchaaksharee Mantra' ('OM NAMAH SHIVAAYA') at least 108 times. This offering should be followed by the 'Abhishekam' (ceremonial bathing of the Lingam) with Panchamritam. "Subsequently the devotee should mediate on my Eight Forms", advised Lord Shiva (while chanting the relevant Mantras as given below]

Mantra	Lingam
SARVAAYA NAMAH	Prithvi (clay) Lingam
BHAVAAYA NAMAH	Jala Lingam
UGRAAYA NAMAH	Vayur Lingam
RUDRAAYA NAMAH	Jyoti Lingam
BHEEMAAYA NAMAH	Akash Lingam
PASHUPATAAYE NAMAH	Yajan Lingam
MAHADEVAAYA NAMAH	Soma Lingam
ISHAAYA NAMAH	Surya Lingam

[All these Lingams are imagined to be formed of the earth, water, light, air, space, sacrificial material, Soma-Creeper and of the sun respectively. Each Mantra should be chanted, imagining these very Lingams as being kept before one].

Then in the first part of the might on Mahashivaratri, the devotee should bathe the Lingam with milk, in the second part with curds, in the third part with ghee and in the fourth-part with honey.

Since a sect of Shaivites believes in the Vaam-Marg Sadhana', they give much emphasis to the 'Beej-Mantras'. [Literally they are 'Seed Incantations' in which much emphasis is placed on their correct pronunciation or the phonetic effect and less on their meanings].

The following Beeja-Mantras should be chanted at the appropriate hours during the Mahashivaratri (night of Lord Shiva) in the following manner:

First part of the night : HREEM ISHAANAAYA NAMAH
Second part of the nigh : HREEM AGHORAAYA NAMAH
Third part of the night : HREEM VAAMDEVAAYA NAMAH
Fourth part of the night : HREEM SAGYOJAATAAYA NAMAH

Besides these, on that auspicious day, in the early morning, one should chant the Beej Mantra: HREEM TATPURUSHAAYA NAMAH.

Finally, after waving of the lighted lamp around the Lingam one should partake of the Panchamritam and the Prasaadam (of the offerings). This fast is the most auspicious one and the ultimate day for the worshipper of Shiva, the Master of Time and Universe.

Rudraksha: The Eye of Rudra

This fruit of the tree of Rudraksha (Utra Swam Bead Tree) is held to be very dear to Rudra or Shiva. Generally found in the jungles of the Valley (of the Himalaya). this tree grows to medium height (6 to 8 feet) and has small round leaves. It is the fruit of this tree which is called Rudraksha (literally. the eye of Rudra). Its other names are Shivaksha and Neela-kanthaksha.

Apart from being very auspicious this bead has superlative medicinal qualities. According to 'Ayurveda' its various concoctions can cure all the bodily ills caused by the disturbance in any of the basic three humours in the body: Vaat (gas), Pitta (bile) and Kapha (phlegm). Since it is believed to be an embodied form of Lord Shiva all the disturbances caused by the evil spirits get automatically quelled if one bears even one of the Rudraksha in a thread. Those affected with neurological disorders must keep this bead or a rosary of it touching their skin. It is believed to be ideal for those suffering from 'Rakta-Chaap' (blood-pressure) related problems. Drinking the water in which few beads have been marinated overnight is a sure cure for all ailments connected with blood impurity disorders. Rubbing these heads in water and then putting the paste over the spots on the skin clears all blemishes of the skin. It has great religious significance as well. The Purana declares that he who wears a Rudraksha becomes almost like Rudra (Shiva) himself and Lord Shiva accepts no worship unless it is accompanied by this divine bead.

BINA BHASMA TRIPUNDENA BINA RUDRAKSHA MAALAYAA

POOJITOAPI MAHADEV NA SYAAT TASYA PHALAPRADAH.

[The worship of Mahadeva brings no fruit if it is not accompanied by the Trident-like sacred mark cast on one's forehead by the holy ash or the garland of Rudraksha bead round one's neck].

The Purana claims that he who keeps Rudraksha near him stays away from all vices, evil spirits and foul pursuits.

This bead or its rosaries can be worn by anybody with- out any distinction of caste, creed, culture or cult but it should be put on a clean body with a heart devoted to Lord Shiva.

That Rudraksha is believed to be of a better quality which is firm, thick, smooth and even in shape. This bead has small grain-like shapes covering the entire space. If rubbed against the touchstone, like gold, it leaves a golden line; real Rudraksha would leave a blackish line.

Although this Purana only refers about a story which is supposed to have been recounted by Lord Shiva himself to his eldest son Shadanana—telling about the origin of this bead, its full account is available in other ancient tomes. When the demons of Tripura had become very powerful and had defeated the gods, the latter had to seek Shiva's help. He knew that he might not be able to slay this demon with his normal weapons, so he started perfecting his special weapon called AGHOR. For this purpose he had to keep his eyes closed for a very long period. This strenuous effort made his eyes ooze a few drops of water (or tears) which fell upon the earth. They created this bead.

These beads are available in many varieties. Their quality is determined by the number of faces upon their body. Their brief description along with their special qualities are given below. These 'faces' are actually the number of holes on the body of the bead.

Among all the beads, the one-faced Rudraksha is deemed to be very auspicious. It is the ultimate-priced object for the aspirant of the 'Vaam-Marg' Sadhana (black-worship). It is believed that he who possesses this kind of Rudraksha has his all mundane and spiritual desires. He never suffers any want and Lord Shiva always keeps his protecting hand over that devotee. 'Ayurveda' gives a small test to ascertain its genuineness: Keep it in a cup full of water for half an hour. It will heat up the water a bit if it is real. The wearer of this bead stays healthy.

Other beads of importance are 'Trimukhi', 'Shadmukhi' and 'Dashmukhi' (three-faced, six-faced and ten-faced respectively). Wearing a black berry rosary in such a way as to make each bead touch the skin has been proved to be very effective cure to all ailments. It keeps the body healthy.

Normally these beads are available in three colours: dark-red, reddish brown and black. The number of the beads in a 'mala' (rosary) must not be less than 108. This number is of great significance as it is believed to cover the entire cosmos.[1]

---

1. Astronomically there are twenty seven asterisms which cover the whole universe. Since each of these asterisms has four 'Charan', 27 × 4 or 108 number covers the entire zodiac, symbolically.

Thousand Names of Lord Shiva

Many eons ago, a fierce war raged between the gods and the demons. The gods received a sound thrashing and fled. While they were running away, they happened to encounter Vishnu. When Vishnu asked the reason and learnt about it, he advised the gods to start praying Lord Tripurari (Shiva) since "only he is capable of subduing these wroth demons". Then saying so Vishnu also joined the gods to invoke Lord Shiva to their presence. Guided by Lord Vishnu they chanted the 1000 names of Lord Shiva. [For convenience all these 1000 names have been grouped in the categories containing 10 names each]. These names are:

1. Gunakaraga, Satyasatyapara, Dina, Dharmaga, Ananda, Dharmasadhana, Anantadrishti, Danda, Damayita, Dama.
2. Abhivadva, Mahamaya, Vishvakarma, Visharada, Vitaraga, Vinitama, Tapasvi, Bhutabhavana, Unmattavesha, Pracchanna.
3. Jitakama, Ajitapriya, Kalyanaprakriti, Kalpa, Sarvalokaprajapati, Tarasvi, Tavaka, Dhimana, Pradhanaprabhu. Avyaya.
4. Lokapala, Antarhitatma. Kalpadi. Kamallekshana, Vedashastrarthatattvajna. Aniyama. Niyatashraya. Chandra. Surya, Shani.
5. Ketu, Varanga, Vidrumaacchavi, Bhaktivashya, Anagha, Parabrahmamrigavanarpana, Adri, Adryalaya, Kanta, Paramatma.
6. Jagadguru, Sarvakarmalaya, Tushta, Mangalya, Mangalavrita, Mahatapa, Dirghatapa, Sthavishtha, Sthavira, Dhruva.
7. Aha, Samvatsara, Vyapti, Pramana, Paramatapa, Samvatsarakara, Mantrapratyayakara, Sarveshvara, Aja, Sarvadarshana.
8. Siddha, Mahareta, Mahabala, Yogi, Yogya, Siddhi, Mahateja, Sarvadi, Agraha, Vasu.

9. Vasumana, Satya. Sarvapapahara, Sukirti. Shobhana, Shrimana, Avanmanasagochara. Amritashashvata, Shanta, Vanahasta.
10. Mridu, Samadhivedya, Kodandi, Nilakantha, Parashvadhi, Vishalaksha, Mrigavyadha, Suresha, Suryatapana, Dharmadhama.
11. Kshamakshetra, Bhagavana, Bhaganetrabhida, Data, Dayakara, Bhava, Savagatah, Purusha, Sarva, Arthitavya.
12. Daksha, Karmandi, Kamashasana. Shmashananilya, Suksha, Shmashanastha, Maheshavara, Lokakarta, Mrigapati, Mahakarta.
13. Mahoushadhi, Uttara, Gopati, Gopta, Jnanagmya, Puratana, Niti, Suniti, Shuddatma, Soma.
14. Somarata, Sukhi, Somapa, Amritapa, Soumya, Mahatejah, Mahadyuti, Tejomaya, Amritamaya, Annamaya.
15. Sudhapati, Ajatshatru, Aloka, Sambhavya, Havyavahana, Lokakara, Vedakara, Sutrakara, Sanatana, Maharshi.
16. Kapilcharya, Vishvadipti, Vilochana, Pinakapani, Bhudeva, Svastida, Svastikrita, Sudhi, Dhatridhama, Dhamakara.
17. Sarvaga, Sarvagochara, Brahmasrika, Vishvasrika, Sarga, Karanikara, Priya, Kavi, Shakha, Vishakha.
18. Goshakha, Shiva, Bhishaka, Anuttama, Gangaplavodaka. Bhavya, Pushkala, Sthapati, Sthira, Vijitatma.
19. Vishayatma, Bhutavahana, Sarathi, Sagana, Ganakaya, Sukirti, Chinnasamshaya Kamadeva, Kamapala, Bhasmoddulita-vigraha.
20. Bhasmapriya, Bhasmashayi, Kami, Kanta, Kritagama, Samavarta, Nivritatma, Dharmapunja, Sadashiva, Akalmasha.
21. Chaturvahu, Durvasa, Durasada, Durlabha, Durgama, Durga, Sarvayudhavisharada, Adhyatmayoganilaya, Sutantu, Tanturvardhana.
22. Shubhanga, Lokasa anga, Jagadisha, Janardana, Bhasmashuddhikara, Meru, Ojasvi, Shuddhavigraha, Asadhya, Sadhusadhya.
23. Bhrityamarkatarupadhrika, Hiranyareta, Pourana,

Ripujivahara, Bala, Mahahrada, Mahagarta, Vyali. Siddhavrindaravandita, Vyaghracharmambara.

24. Shiva, Hara Mrida, Rudra, Pushkara, Pushpalochana, Arthigamya, Sadachara, Sharva, Shambhu.

25. Maheshvara, Chandrapida, Chandramouli, Vishva, Vishvamareshvara, Vedantasarasandoha, Kapil, Nilalohita, Dhyanadhara, Aparicchedya.

26. Gouribharta, Ganeshvara, Ashtamurti, Vishvamurti, Trivargasvargasadhana, Jnanagamya, Dridaprajna, Devadeva, Trilochana, Vamadeva.

27. Mahadeva, Patu, Parvrida, Drida, Vishvarupa, Virupaksha, Vagisha, Shuchisattama, Sarvapramanasamvadi, Vrishanka.

28. Vrishavahana, Isha, Pinaki, Khatvanga, Chitravesha, Chirantana, Tamohara, Mahayogi, Gopta, Brahma.

29. Dhurjati, Kalakala, Krittivasah, Subhaga, Pranavatmaka, Unnadhra, Purusha, Jushya, Durvasa, Purashasana.

30. Divyayudha, Skandaguru, Parameshthi, Paratpara, Anadimadhyanidhana, Girisha, Girijadhava, Kuberabandhu, Shrikantha, Lokavarnottama.

31. Mahabhuta, Mahanidhi, Amirtasha, Amritavapu, Panchajanya, Prabhanjana, Panchavimshatitattvastha, Parijata, Para-uara, Sulabha.

32. Suvrata, Shura, Brahmavedanidhi, Nidhi, Varnashramaguru, Varni, Shatrujita, Shatrutapana, Ashrama, Kshapana.

33. Kshama, Jnanavana, Achaleshvara, Pramanabhuta, Durjneya, Suparna, Vayvahana, Dhanurdhara, Dhanurveda, Gunarashi.

34. Guruda, Lalita, Abheda, Bhavatmatmasamsthita, Vireshvara, Vyavasaya, Vyavasthana, Hara Jagdiya, Param.

35. Virabhadra, Virasanavidhi, Virata, Virachudamani, Vetta, Tivrananda, Nadidhara, Ajnadhara, Trishuli, Shipivishta.

36. Shivalaya, Balakhilya, Mahachapa, Tigmamshu, Badhira, Khaga, Adhirama, Susharana, Subrahmanya, Sudhapati.

37. Maghavana, Koushika, Gomana, Virama, Sarvasadhana, Lalataksha, Vishvadeha, Sara,

Samsarachakrabhrita, Amoghadanda.

38. Madhyastha, Hiranya, Brahmavarchasi, Paramartha, Para, Mayi, Shambara, Vyaghralochana, Ruchi, Virinchi.

39. Svarbandhu, Vachaspati, Aharpati, Ravi, Virochana, Skanda, Shasta, Vaivasvata, Yama, Yukti.

40. Unnatakiriti, Sanuraga, Paranjaya, Kailashadhipati, Kanta, Savita, Ravilochana, Vidvattama, Vitabhaya, Vishabharta.

41. Anivarita, Nitya, Niyatakalyana, Punyashravanakirtana, Durashrava, Vishvasaha, Dhyeya, Duhsvapnanashana, Uttarana, Dushkritiha.

42. Vijneya, Duhsaha, Bhava, Anadi, Bhurbhuvakshi, Kiriti, Ruchirangada, Janana, Janajanmadi, Pritimana.

43. Paratapvana, Kamadalundhara, Dhanvi, Vedanga, Vedavita, Muni, Bhrajihnu, Bhojana, Bhokta, Lokantha.

44. Duradhara, Atindriya, Mahamaya, Sarvavasa, Chatushpatha, Kalayogi, Mahanada, Mahotsaha, Mahabala, Mahabuddhi.

45. Mahavirya, Bhutachari, Purandara, Nishachara, Pretachari, Mahashakti, Mahadyuti, Ahiraeshyavapu, Shrimana, Sarvacharyamanogati.

46. Vahushtuta, Niyatatma, Dhruva, Adhruva, Sarvashaska, Ojastejodyutidhara, Nartaka, Nritypriya, Nrityanitya, Prakashatma.

47. Prakashaka, Spashtakshara, Budha, Mantra, Samana, Sarasamplava Yugadikrida, Yugavarta, Gambhira, Vrishavahana.

48. Ishta, Vishishta, Shishteshta, Shalabha, Sharabha, Dhanu, Tirtharupa, Tirthanama, Tirthadrishya, Stuta.

49. Arthada, Apamnidhi, Adhishthana, Vijaya, Jayakalavita, Pratishthita, Pramanajana, Hiranyakavacha, Hari, Vimochana.

50. Hiranyagarbha, Druhina, Bhutapala, Bhupati, Sadyogi, Yogavit, Yogi, Varada, Brahmanapriya, Devapriya.

51. Devanatha, Devajana, Devachintaka, Vishamksha, Vishalaksha, Vrishada, Vrishavardhana, Nirmama, Nirahamkara, Nirmoha.

52. Nirupadrava, Darpaha, Darpada, Drita, Sarvabhutaparivartaka, Sahasrajit, Saharарchi,

Prabhava, Snigddhaprakritidakshina, Bhutabhavyabhavannatha.

53. Bhutinashana, Artha, Anartha, Mahakosha, Parakaryaikapandita, Nishkantaka, Kirtananda, Nirvyaja, Vyajamardana, Sattvavana.

54. Sattvika, Satyakirti, Snehakritagama, Akampita, Gungrahi, Naikatma, Naikakarmakrit, Suprita, Sumukha, Suksha.

55. Sukara, Dakshinanila, Nandiskandhadhara, Dhurya, Prakata, Pritvardhana, Aparajita, Sarvasattva, Govinda, Adhrita.

56. Sattvavahana, Svadhia, Siddha, Putamurti, Yashodhana, Varahabhringadhrika, Bhringi, Balavana, Ekanayaka, Shrutiprakasha.

57. Shrutimana, Ekabandhu, Anekakrit, Shrivatsalashivarambha, Shantabhadra, Sama, Yasha; Bhushaya, Bhushana, Sthanada.

58. Suragana, Vidyesha, Vindusamshraya, Balarupa, Vikarta, Balonmatta, Gahana, Guha, Karana, Karta.

59. Sakala, Nishkala, Anagha, Akala, Sakaladhara, Pandurabha, Mrida, Nata Purna, Purayita.

60. Punya, Sukumara, Sulochana, Samageyapriya, Akrura, Punyakirti, Anamaya, Manojava, Tirthakara, Jatila.

61. Jiviteshvara, Jivitantakara, Nitya, Vasureta, Vasuprada, Sadgati, Satkriti, Siddhi, Sajjati, Kalakantaka.

62. Kaladhara, Mahakala, Bhutasatyaparayana, Lokalavanyakartta, Lokottarasukhalaya, Chandrasanjivana, Shasta, Lokaguda, Mahadia, Lokabandhu.

63. Lokanatha, Kritajna, Krittibhuyshana, Anapaya, Akshara, Kanta, Sarvashastrabhudvara, Tejomaya, Dyutidhara, Lokagrani.

64. Anu, Shuchismita, Prasannatnia, Durjjeya, Duratikrama, Jyotirmaya, Jagannatha, Nirakara, Jaleshvara, Tumbavma.

65. Mahakopa, Vishoka, Shokanashana, Trilokapa, Trilokesha, Sarvashuddhi, Adhokshaja, Avyaktalakshnana, Deva, Vyaktavyakta.

66. Vishampati, Varashila, Varaguna, Saramandhana, Maya, Brahma, Vishnu, Prajapala, Hamsa, Hanmsagati.

67. Vaya, Vedha, Vidhata, Dhata, Srashta, Harta, Chaturmukha, Kailasashikharavasi, Sarvavasi, Sadagati.
68. Unishpanna, Surabhi, Shishiratmaka, Vasanta, Madhava, Grishma, Nabhasya, Vijavahana, Angira, Guru.
69. Atreya, Vimala, Vishvavahana, Pavana, Sumati, Vidvana, Travidya, Naravahana, Manobuddhi, Ahamkara.
70. Kshetrajna, Kshetrapalaka, Jammadagni, Balanidhi, Vigalal, Vishvagalava, Aghora, Anuttara, Yajna, Shreya.
71. Nishreyahpatha, Shaila, Gaganakundabha, Danavari, Arindama, Rajanijanaka, Charuvishalya, Lokakalpadhrika, Chaturveda, Chatrubhava.
72. Chatura, Chaturapriya, Amlaya, Samamlaya, Tirthaveda-shivalaya, Vahurupa, Maharupa, Sarvarupa, Charachara, Nyayanirmayaka.
73. Nyayi, Nyayagamya, Nirantara, Sahasramurddha, Devendra, Sarvashastraprabhanjana, Munda, Virupa, Vikranta, Dandi.
74. Danta, Gunottama, Pingalaksha, Janadhyaksha, Nilagriva, Niramaya, Sahasravahu, Sarvesha, Sharanaya, Sarvalokadhrika.
75. Padmasana, Paramjyoti, Parampara, Paramfala, Padmagarbha, Mahagarbha, Vishvagarbha, Vichakshana, Characharajna, Varada.
76. Varesha, Mahabala, Devasuraguru, Deva, Devaura-mahashraya, Devadideva, Devagni, Devagnisukhada, Prabhu, Devasureshvara.
77. Divya, Devasuramaheshvara, Devadevamaya, Achintya, Devadevatamasambhava, Sadyoni, Asuravyaghra, Devasimha, Divakara, Vibhudhagravara.
78. Shreshtha, Sarvadevottamottama, Shivajnanarata, Shrimana, Shikhi-Shriparvatapriya, Vajrashasta, Siddhakhadgi, Narasimhanipatana, Brahmachari, Lokachari.
79. Dharmachari Dhandhipa, Nandi, Nandishvara, Ananta, Nagnavratadhara, Shuchi, Lingadhyaksha, Suradhyaksha, Yogadhyaksha.
80. Yugavaha, Svadharma, Svargata, Svargakhara, Svaramayasvana, Vanadhyaksha, Vijakarta,

Dharmakrit, Dharmasabhava, Dambha.

81. Alobha, Arthavit, Shambhu, Sarvabhutamaheshvara, Shmashananilaya, Tryksha, Setu, Apratimakriti, Lokottaras-phutaloka, Trymbaka.

82. Nagabhushana, Andhakari, Makhadveshi, Vishnukandharapatana, Dhurjati, Khandaparshu, Papahari, Akarti Hara, Rudra.

83. Nitimana, Dhava, Vasishtha, Kashyapa, Bhanu, Bhima, Bhimaparakrama, Pranava, Salpatchachara, Mahakasha.

84. Mahaghana, Janmadhipa, Mahadeva, Sakalagamaparaga, Tattva, Tattavit, Ekatma, Vibhu, Vishvavibhushana, Rishi.

85. Brahmana, Aishvaryajanmanrityujaratiga, Panchayajnasamutpatti, Vishvesha, Vimalodaya, Atmayoni, Vatsala, Bhaktalokadhrika, Gayatrivallabha, Anayanta.

86. Pramshu, Vishvavasa, Prabhakara, Shishu, Girirata, Samrata, Sushena, Surashatruha, Amogha, Arishtanemi.

87. Kumuda, Vigatajvara, Svayamjyoti, Tanujyoti, Achanchala, Atamajyoti, Pingala, Kapliashmashru, Bhalanetra, Trayitanu.

88. Jnanaskandarnahaniti, Vishvotpatti, Upadlava, Bhaga, Vivasvana, Aditya, Yogapara, Divaspati, Kalyangunanama, Papaha.

89. Punyadarshana, Udarakirti, Udyogi, Sadyogi, Sadasanmaya, Nakshatramali, Divaspati, Nakesha, Svadhishthanapadashraya, Pavitra.

90. Manipura, Nabhogati, Hrit, Pundarikasina, Shatru, Shranta, Vrishakapi, Ushna, Grihapati, Krishna.

91. Paramartha, Anarthanashana, Adharmashatru, Ajneya, Puruhuta, Purushruta, Brahmagarbha, Vrihadgarbha, Dharmadhenu Dhanagama.

92. Jagaddhitaishi, Sugata, Kumara, Kushalagama, Hiranyavarna, Jyotishmana, Nanabhutarata, Dhvani, Araga, Nayanadhyaksha.

93. Vishvamitra, Dhaneshvara, Brahmajyoti, Vasudhama, Mahajyotianuttama, Matamaha, Matarishva, Nabhasvana, Nagaharadhrika, Pulastya.

94. Pulaha, Agastya, Jalukarnya, Parashara,

Niravarananirvara, Vairanchya, Vishtarashrava, Atmabhu, Aniruaddha, Atri.

95. Jnananmurti, Mahayasha, Lokaviragrani, Vira, Chanda, Satyaparakrama, Vyalakalpa, Mahakalpa, Kalpaviriksha, Kaladhara.

96. Alankarishnu, Achala, Rochishnu, Vikramonnata, Ayuhshabdapati, Vegi, Plavana, Shikhisarathi, Asamsrishta, Atithi.

97. Shatrupreamathi, Padapasana, Vasushrava, Pratapa, Havyavaha, Vishvabhojana, Japaya, Jaradishamana, Lohitatma, Tanunapata.

98. Vrihadashva, Nabhoyoni, Supratika, Tamisraha, Nidagha, Tapana, Megha, Svaksha, Parapuranjaya, Sukhanila.

99. Vivikshu, Visharada, Shubda, Shubha, Karta, Shubhanama, Shobhan, Anarthita, Ageena, Sakshi.

100. Parathavritti, Nityashantiparayana, Mahatyagi, Satyavrata, Nilalohita, Kaleha, Bhakti Raja, Akampa Bhootabhavana, Bhutakriti.

1. It is apparent that some names have been repeated and some are also the epithets used for other super-gods. But some common names have different meanings by Sanskrit grammar which vary according to the context they are used in.